*Wisdom of the Wealthy*

# WISDOM OF THE WEALTHY

## Conversations on *Transmuting Challenges* into *Millions*

## DR. TABREZ SHERIFF, MD

**Wisdom Wealth**
PUBLISHING

WISDOM OF THE WEALTHY
*Conversations on Transmuting Challenges into Millions*

ISBN 978-1-5445-2110-7 *Hardcover*
978-1-5445-2109-1 *Paperback*
978-1-5445-2108-4 *Ebook*
978-1-5445-2111-4 *Audiobook*

*Dedicated to:*

*1) A person in pursuit of his/her American Dream*

*2) Every hardworking American*

*3) Every immigrant who makes this country great*

# CONTENTS

# INTRODUCTION

This book contains the collective life experiences and perspectives of three immigrants who came to the United States broke but are now millionaires. I have tried my level best to explain their ideas. These ideas will help you formulate a successful mindset and help you build wealth and success.

Some of the concepts may seem counterintuitive at first glance, but they've been tried and tested by the wealthy. I will introduce them to you. Believe me; these concepts have the highest probability of achieving success for you. While reading this book, you will probably see something that resonates. I am congratulating you, in the present, for your millionaire status in the future. If you were born in the US or arrived here as an immigrant and are still not successful, you probably need to read this book. It will walk you through and teach you how to transmute success by diverting and channeling energy from your personal challenges.

If you already are successful, then this book will help you harness all your energy to achieve far greater success and prosperity.

This book will teach you how to build wealth. It will demonstrate strategies, by using examples, with the ultimate goal of helping you become successful and financially free.

What does *wealth* mean? Wealth is not just about making money. It's about creating a life in a manner that allows you not to have to work for money to live. Creating enough wealth means living a wonderful life and not having to worry about a job that you may lose someday. Life is about creating more time for yourself, by eliminating unnecessary tasks that prevent you from living life in the manner you want to live it. One of the most unwanted, time-consuming tasks in every human life is running around a clock, at work, to generate money to then live a life.

Wealth simply means having enough money working for you to pay your bills and all expenses, whether you choose to work or not.

So how is being wealthy different from being rich? It can be simply explained as follows: if you can save money, pay all your expenses, and enjoy your life, then you are already rich. When you no longer need to exchange your time to earn money, and when this money is sufficient to pay for all your life's expenses, needs, and enjoyments in perpetuity, then you are wealthy.

Assets are things that pay you, and liabilities are things that cost you money.

For example, if you earned $200 a month and spent $100 a month on all expenses, and were left with $100 for fun things in life, then chances are you might already be rich.

However, if you owned a property or stocks/bonds (assets) that paid you rent/dividend/interest, etc. (asset income), equal to $200, and you spent the same $100 on expenses, and the other $100 to enjoy life, then chances are you are wealthy.

You see, for the first scenario, you were working, but in the second scenario, your assets worked for you, and you got paid $200, whether you worked or not.

This book will not only help you build wealth; it will also help you find purpose in life. You will turn your challenges into success by using the methods described in this book.

The wisdom of the wealthy will guide you toward the correct method of investing, help you avoid pitfalls, and prevent you from being exploited by pundits (self-proclaimed experts looking to steal your money).

*Disclaimer: the reader may choose to follow or not follow advice mentioned in this book at his or her own free will. The author takes no responsibility for changes in behavior, sexual preference, investment choices, or their performance. This book is not meant to advise you on specific investments, but is intended to help you learn about some common and uncommon techniques of investing that will help you build long-term wealth. Furthermore, this advice is not the only means of achieving success, financial independence, or building wealth. This book is a collection of personal experiences, ideas, and wisdom. It is not to be considered an expert opinion on topics discussed or for financial/investment advice.*

*Chapter 1*

# FIND YOUR WHY

A camping trip changed my life. What I thought would be a weekend getaway of fishing and campfire stories at the Lake of the Woods in Northern Minnesota ended up being the start of a total financial transformation in my life. I went on the trip with three physician colleagues who'd become close friends, three very wealthy colleagues who shared their journeys and wisdom with me. I still implement the lessons I learned on that trip.

We camped by a warm fire under a cool, summer night sky. Holding coffee mugs, we gazed at the stars and the northern lights.

There was Masood, with his sharp nose in the dim campfire light, sipping his coffee. Apart from being a physician, he was also an inventor and had several patents in his name. His first patent was filed, during medical school, on an improvement he made to the central line catheter. He predicted that it would become the standard of care many years from now. His professors and colleagues made fun of him and, sometimes, called him crazy. This man sitting in front of me, sipping his coffee, was indeed crazy, not the type on medications, but the type Steve Jobs often spoke of.

And then there was Ravi, tall with a big, hairy head that seemed too heavy for his thin neck, and a nose curved twenty degrees to his left. Ravi was not just an intensivist but also a rock star at investing. He created his wealth through the practice of medicine and by investing in the stock market. We studied at the same school in India, but I didn't know him well enough then, and we only became close friends after I met him in the United States. Though I didn't know him well in college, I knew this about him: there was no soul, in the entire college, who could compete with him. His exam scores, during all of our years in college, were near perfect. Ravi never spoke much, but during college days, there was one rule that everyone followed without disagreement: when Ravi spoke, everyone listened.

And finally, there was Mervin, with perfectly chiseled, manicured facial hair, with a pierced left earlobe and visible scars on his neck and wrists. He was a hospitalist who became very wealthy by investing his savings in real estate. I met him when I was a hospitalist working at a rural hospital in a small town in northern Minnesota called Bemidji. Mervin was an independent contractor with Masood's hospitalist staffing company. He was a party animal, with a right balance of focus and fun. He shared his challenges with me and showed how one could live a purposeful life fulfilling someone else's dream. It was his path to success and secret to financial freedom.

We chatted and bantered about every random thing that popped into our heads. I was the odd one, not as wealthy as these guys, but I was curious to know what made them so wealthy. This was my opportunity to understand how their thought process worked. I wanted to learn from them. I wanted financial freedom for myself.

Just like me, Masood, Ravi, and Mervin were immigrants from India. But they were far wealthier and more successful than most people in the United States.

I decided to ask a few questions, to hear Masood's story in his own words. Masood started sharing his story.

Masood said, "We were so poor that my father could barely pay my school fees." When Masood came to America, as an adult, he had $200 in his pocket. He lived on Caesar salads, since that's all he could afford.

After a few years in the United States, he became a millionaire and then went on to create more prosperity and happiness for himself and his family in the United States and India.

"It's not magic," he told us. "It's a blueprint that anyone can apply, and it resides in every person's heart and mind. It may take you a little more time, or less, but you will get there too."

## MASOOD'S WHY: NO POOR PATIENT LEFT BEHIND

"I vividly recall my sixth-grade year in India," Masood said. What followed was a description so detailed, it was as though he was still living it. "I remember wearing my school uniform and sitting beside my grandfather, who lay in a hospital bed with chest pain. My school shorts were old and torn at the back. But you couldn't tell they were torn, unless you focused on it, because my mother stitched them up so well. The shoulder straps of my old school backpack were torn too, so I improvised and tied them together. I covered the knots with my hands when I walked around.

"My feet ached every day, because my shoes were too small and too tight, and it was not unusual for me to be forced to stand outside the classroom because of unpaid fees." Masood paused and stretched out his feet, staring at his expensive shoes, which reflected the campfire light. He sighed. "I never complained, of course, because I was grateful to my father, who worked very hard to make ends meet.

"That day in the hospital, I'd stood outside for at least three hours, and I could feel the agony of my toes deforming. But my worry for my grandfather hurt even more." Back at the hospital, he remembered, his grandfather reached out and took his hand. He said, "I still remember the warmth of his big, comfortable palm as he reassured me that everything would be OK."

"I am just waiting for the doctor to come see me," his grandfather told him. "The doctor will get me healthy again, and then we will all be on our way home."

Masood's grandfather was still in an immense amount of pain. His chest still hurt, and no doctor had come to see him yet. It had been more than a day since he was admitted to a hospital, but no doctor would see him because Masood's family was so poor. They could not afford the doctor's fee.

Doctor after doctor would walk by, and his old grandmother would run to them, begging them for help.

"*Sahib, bade sahib* (respected sir, big, respected sir)," she would say. "Please take a look at my husband. We are arranging some money and we will pay you soon." But Masood's family had no money.

After a whole day of running around, she would sit, quietly sobbing on the stairway at the hospital entrance. Masood's father, her son, spent every minute of that day at the doorsteps of several people who promised to loan him some money but did not deliver on that promise. In their eyes, Masood's family was not simply broke or poor. They were the dirt on the streets of India that had no value.

While holding his hand, Masood's grandfather asked him, "What did you learn in school today?"

Masood confessed that he'd once again stood outside his math class, not allowed to enter because the previous month's school fees were not paid. He could not see what the teacher wrote on the blackboard, but he heard everything she taught.

"Do you remember the story of the ant and the big hill?" his grandfather asked.

Little Masood nodded and began to recite: "The ant is a tiny creature, with tiny eyes, but a massive vision. The ant looks at the hill nearby and says, 'I will climb to the top someday.' All the other ants make fun of him, nobody believes it, and they ridicule him as he trips, falls, and fails a million times...and then one day, the ant climbs to the top of the hill."

His grandfather listened carefully, eyes closed, with the hint of a smile on his lips. But he didn't say anything, and Masood assumed he was very tired. A short while later, he went home with his mother, but his father stayed at the hospital.

The following day, he went to school and was made to stand outside the classroom again. His classmates teased him every time this happened; it was embarrassing and difficult, at first, but he learned to develop a thick skin, at a young age.

Masood returned to the hospital, the next day after school, and was shocked to find his grandfather's condition had rapidly deteriorated. His grandfather was barely opening his eyes, his face was pale, and there was dark pigmentation under his lower eyelids. That shine he always carried in his eyes seemed to have disappeared. His lips were purple.

"Did the doctor come to see you?" Masood asked. There was no answer. His grandmother, who was wiping the beads of sweat off her husband's forehead with the end of her sari (a traditional woman's garment), shook her head. Yet another doctor passed by the door, and she ran to him for help.

Masood tried to have a conversation with his grandfather, but his hand seemed cold, and he would not talk. He appeared to mumble, but Masood could barely hear what he was saying or make sense of it. Intuitively, the young Masood knew something was very wrong, and a strange pain overcame him. Masood felt a squeeze in his chest, and his eyes flooded with tears.

He looked at the monitor, which had been connected only after what seemed to be the millionth request of his grandmother. Lines zigzagged, accompanied by rapid beeping. Masood froze in fear. Suddenly, the line went flat, and his grandfather simply lay there, staring at the ceiling.

Masood screamed.

Hearing the scream, both grandmother and the doctor came running. After an examination, the doctor expressed sadness, declared the patient dead, and said that it may have been a heart attack.

"Just like, that he died," Masood told us. "Just like that..." It was evident that time had not alleviated his aching heart.

The aftermath was a flood of agony. His grandmother screamed and beat her chest and head with her palms, while other patients, along with their poor families in the medical ward, witnessed this tragedy. They all shared one thing in common—they were all extremely poor.

Years later, on a camping trip under the stars, Masood looked at us and asked, "Do you know what happens to a poor person in a poor country when they can't see a doctor?"

We simply looked at him, tears in our eyes.

Masood answered his own question, in a soft voice: "They die. They die..."

## THE CREATOR'S WHISPER: A PERSON'S WHY

The day Masood's grandfather died, Masood made a promise to himself that never again would a beloved member of any family die in a similar manner, that, one day, he would connect the whole globe; he vowed that every person on this planet would have access to a physician, irrespective of their financial situation. It was a big dream for a little kid with a torn uniform, but it was the fuel that stirred the fire in his gut.

Masood, with crooked toes (deformed from ill-fitting shoes as a kid), went from wearing a torn uniform to starting and running a successful physician-staffing company with millions in revenue. He runs thirty-six charity health clinics in India. He not only performs free cardiac catheterizations and treats heart disease, but he also provides free medical aid to more than one million families below the poverty line.

Today, he is an asset to all Americans and the underprivileged in India. The world needs more Masoods.

To date, Masood's grandfather is still his greatest source of inspiration. Sitting next to the campfire, he admitted to sometimes wondering, "Would I still be a physician if my grandfather did not die that day?"

Perhaps not. Perhaps everything happens for a reason. Maybe it was nature's way of ensuring that millions of lives were healed through his hands.

Pain can be an agent of change, especially when you have lost something so valuable. When you know something so important is never coming back, it changes you.

When faced with a challenge, remember that difficulties have always induced evolution. You either adapt and evolve, or perish. Masood knew that standing outside classrooms would not make him a doctor. He had to evolve and be innovative and resourceful. For instance, with three families living under one roof, it was difficult for him to study. Fortunately, a bright streetlight outside his house provided both light and quiet for him to read after sunset.

Under the streetlight he would imagine himself, in great detail, as a physician treating patients and performing imaginary surgeries on imaginary patients. He would try to imagine the feel of a suture in his hand and try to feel its consistency as he tied a knot while closing an imaginary surgical incision. This kept him going.

Many of Masood's classmates excelled because of help from their parents or by attending tutoring sessions after school. He couldn't rely on learning from his mother, a fourth-grade dropout who didn't know English, and he definitely couldn't afford a tutor. He dedicated hours, each day, to studying, looking up the answers to questions and figuring out the in-between steps that would take him from a question to an answer. And no matter what, he showed up to school, every single day, even when the teachers sent him outside because he couldn't pay his fees. What were they going to do, lock the school gates? The way he looked at it, he did not have the luxury to drop out of school—and later, college. If you cannot demonstrate your commitment toward your choices, then you cannot be trusted to continue to commit to your choices. Masood had nothing to lose and everything to gain.

Remember, the human mind has no limitations. Whenever the human will is pushed to its limits, the mind innovates. Whenever Masood faltered, he would be consumed by fear—fear of an unfulfilled dream and of not being able to fulfill the promise he had made to himself.

When fear is at its peak, the best way to tackle it is to force your mind into productive distractions. This is when innovation happens. Look at your challenges with a fresh perspective. Treat them as things that can only lift you upward.

If the human mind is pushed to its limits, then, generally, evolution occurs at the point of maximum discomfort.

You will never read this in any book, and no person of success will share it with you. This, my friend, is the secret. No person of success did it all by himself or herself. Each and every one of them had something—or someone—that stood as their source of energy in times of great despair.

Masood calls it the "Creator's Whisper." It is a person's true purpose; it's what the creator wants them to do. Successful people live and breathe their purpose. The creator whispers in a person's mind and shows them visions of who they really are, who they should become: the reason for their creation.

*Blessed rather are those who hear the word of God and obey it. (Luke 11:28)*

Great leaders, philosophers, and saints search for this whisper, sometimes by isolating themselves and meditating until they attain clarity of purpose: Gautama Buddha under a peepal tree; Prophet Mohammed in a cave; Prophet Moses on a mountain. In modern times, Bill Gates isolates himself in his cabin. Steve Jobs practiced meditation at home. Even Ray Dalio meditates on a daily basis. If you thought there was nothing common among all great and successful people, then think again!

Those who think deeply and meditate develop a strong pathway toward this whisper and call it "intuition." Of course, there are some who don't meditate but still hear the whisper, but generally, the lesser the worldly noise, confusion, or distraction, the better. Typically, the more successful a person is, the stronger their ability to hear the whisper and block out other people's opinions.

*Don't let the noise of others' opinions drown out your own inner voice. And most important, have the courage to follow your heart and intuition, they somehow already know what you truly want to become. Everything else is secondary. (Steve Jobs)*

The ability to tune in to the Creator's Whisper resides in each one of us. We are simply deaf to it. Once discovered, it's a person's choice to listen to it, through power of reason and imagination, or to listen to the noise on this planet. Think about the people you hear complaining about their bills, their nine-to-five jobs, and being stuck doing what they never wanted to do. Did all those people listen to other people? This is precisely why many thinkers and successful people spend time in isolation, reflecting on their purpose in life and then going after that whisper with all their might.

Masood heard his Creator's Whisper under a streetlamp, in isolation. Today he is a very successful physician saving millions of lives.

It is easy to wonder if successful people are simply special, with magical abilities. But you just read the story of Masood. His life was painful. He had experienced more pain and embarrassment as a child than one can imagine. He worked his mental muscles for years, slowly and steadily surpassing his peers, imagining his future life as a physician helping those in need.

I am reminded of a story Masood once shared, of him observing a man working in a quarry. The man kept striking at a stone, with a tiny hammer, and even though it had no effect on the stone, he kept doing it over and over again. After the hundredth or so strike, the stone cracked. He told the man that the last strike must have been the best one, since it cracked the stone, to which the worker replied, "It was not the last one, but all the strikes before it."

I have come to believe success is not a special trait or a special gene inherited at birth. Success is what a person makes of themself, a person who has found their why.

Masood wasn't the only one with such a powerful why. Once he shared his story, Ravi and Mervin began to open up as well.

## RAVI'S WHY: UNREQUITED LOVE

The campfire dwindled, but Mervin rekindled it with more wood. Wolves howled in the distance. As a cool breeze blew, Ravi reached for another beer. Masood sipped on the same coffee he'd been sipping the whole evening. Mervin poked at the fire, and I reached for some delicious walleye filet.

We'd been processing Masood's words, in silence, when Ravi suddenly smiled and said, "You know, Masood, all this talk of the Creator's Whisper and finding our whys...I think I know mine. My story isn't too different from yours.

"I had four pairs of clothes, and I wore them for two years during medical school. I was not even fortunate to have a father to beg for new clothes. During college, I worked at a bowling alley, and during medical school, I helped a family doctor at his clinic. This allowed me to pay my fees and care for my aging mother. I never realized people observe what clothes you wear. I only became conscious of this fact when she first noticed it and asked me if I had no clothes."

"She!" Masood exclaimed.

Masood had been talking about things that made us what we are, things that drove us, things that made us persist through adversity and find success. Ravi never seemed comfortable speaking about his life, but hearing Masood may have motivated him. Perhaps we were about to learn Ravi's why.

"Ravi, tell us about her," I said, gently.

Ravi shook his head, cleared his throat, and began his tale.

Ravi lost his father when he was in the eleventh grade, and so, responsibility fell on his shoulders from a very young age. He not only had to study, but also work, pay rent, and take care of his aging mother. His father died of pneumonia; he kept coughing, for weeks, until he started coughing up blood.

His family was dirt poor, and he could only afford to commute, via public bus, from home to medical school. On one occasion, he ran into his old school English teacher, who happened to be on the same bus. That teacher had bullied him, because he kept failing his English tests, and had insisted that Ravi would amount to nothing in life.

To make class more exciting, the teacher made him stand in front of the class while other classmates openly estimated when his shirt was last washed or the last time he had a bath. It was humiliating, and little Ravi thought he'd die from shame. Once, he was even forced to kneel down, in front of the whole class, because his shoes were dirty. The teacher pulled his long hair into a *juttu* (ponytail) as the entire class watched and ridiculed. Ravi was the joke of that class.

Ravi did not have the heart to explain these school experiences to his parents. His parents never had the money to buy shoe polish or take him to the barber.

Several years later, on the bus, his teacher immediately recognized him. When Ravi's stop arrived and he was ready to get off the bus, the teacher asked, "Is this bus stop close to your home?"

"No, it's close to the medical school," Ravi replied.

The teacher, astonished, asked, "You are a medical student?"

"Yes," he replied.

Indeed, Ravi had cracked one of the toughest competitive exams in India and gotten into medical school. The government agreed to pay his fees because of his exceptional scores.

"What changed?" asked the teacher, who never thought Ravi, of all students, was so capable.

Ravi smiled and replied, "Every morning I would walk to school, and I would see you get off the bus. Then you would take the bus home every evening. You always complained about the government, the climate, the economy, and life, during our English classes. Students say you still do, and you ask students for donations and talk about your money issues at home. I knew I was your least favorite student because I never had any money to give. Growing up, I just did not want to be like you."

But while not growing up to become like his English teacher motivated him, Ravi's why was actually "someone" else.

"Brinda," Ravi told us around the campfire, whispering her name as if it was sacred.

During his college days he took an evening job at a bowling alley, to earn money to take care of his mother. He studied at college, during the day, and worked in the evening. This was the toughest time of his life. The only light at the end of the tunnel was Brinda, his classmate. She was the only reason he didn't drop out. He would arrive at college early, simply to catch a glimpse of her when she walked into the classroom.

She was the most beautiful girl Ravi had ever seen, and he deeply admired her, more than admired—he was absolutely crazy about her and everything she did. He would wait outside places where she would likely hang out, thereby improving his chances of striking up a conversation. He found out which neighborhood she lived in, which library she went to, and where her mother shopped for groceries. In his heart, he believed that he would marry her one day.

He was not rich enough to afford a vehicle or gadgets to get her attention, nor was he attractive or "date-worthy," in his words. The first time she ever looked at him was when the professor asked a question that no one answered but him.

After that, Ravi assumed that if he answered all questions in class, she would notice him more and turn to him with questions in math or science. Helping her might lead to a conversation and possibly a date. He worked extra hard in the evenings and stayed up all night reading every chapter, in detail, that was to be taught the following day, all for potentially being noticed by the person he admired most.

Eventually, he rose to the top of the class, answering every question and scoring the highest on tests, not because he wanted to excel academically, but because he wanted the girl to notice him. As days and months passed, Brinda started to ask him questions about science, which motivated him more. He worked even harder to get her attention in class, to the extent that he got absolutely perfect scores. On some occasions, he knew more than the teachers on the subject.

My friend had turned into something that he had never imagined; he went from zero (failing in English classes) to an absolute hero (superhuman), all for a girl whom he admired and revered from the bottom of his heart. If love was so powerful, could it transform every loser, if channeled correctly? Ravi had somehow transmuted his love and devotion toward Brinda onto his education.

If Ravi had not fallen in love with Brinda, he would not have finished college. If not for the transmutation, he would not have the ability to not only crack but also top the competitive exams, after college, to get into medical school.

Ravi stopped, left the empty beer bottle and grabbed some coffee from the pot. He had woken up his aching heart. Pulling his eyebrows close to his upper eyelids, he paused. The wrinkles on his forehead straightened out.

It was clear that he was having a very difficult time telling us the rest of the story. Mervin tried to offer some support. He walked over to Ravi and gently rested his hand on his shoulder. We could all recognize the pain of a broken heart on Ravi's face.

Ravi's story did not have a happy ending. During the final year of college, he spotted Brinda with the best-looking guy in class. She sat in the front seat of a blue car, a car that belonged to the best-looking boy's father.

Ravi was devastated, and he felt as if someone had ripped his heart out. Brinda was the only ray of hope and happiness in his life. Ravi had already lost his father a few years earlier. He attended college during the day, worked in the evening, and studied at night. He pushed himself beyond what was humanly possible and persisted through it. He did it just to look at Brinda at college, and that brought relief and peace to his painful world.

Ravi spent the rest of the day in self-analysis, feeling like a failure. This was a double punch. First his father had passed away, a few years earlier, and he had all the responsibilities on his shoulders. Now he was heartbroken and had failed in love. As he headed to the bus stop, he looked at the shirt and pants he'd been wearing for the last three days and his worn-out slippers. He thought about that shiny blue car. There was no way he could afford such a car. And there was no way he could ever look like that fair-skinned, handsome guy. He despised his darker skin color (unfortunately fair skin is still considered more attractive than dark skin in India) and crooked nose. Why did nature decide to create him so unattractive? He got off the bus, furious with nature, but did not go home. Instead, he went to a park nearby, trekked up a hill, and watched the sun go down. His pockets had never felt so empty.

As the sun set, Ravi told himself, "This world is unfair; I stand no chance. I do not have what it takes to date a girl whom I absolutely love more than anything in this world. The only thing I can give her is my life, because that is all I have."

But what was his life worth then anyway?

Then came his decision: he would tell the girl how he felt about her, no matter what. The following day, Ravi approached Brinda and professed his love. He promised her that, though he had nothing, he would be very successful and wealthy one day.

Brinda listened politely, but revealed that what mattered to her was a comfortable life, which only a wealthy person could provide. She liked the guy she was dating, though admitted Ravi was very hardworking. She respected the fact that Ravi would do anything for her but said, "Ravi, maybe you should first figure out how to make some money and buy new clothes, before asking a girl out. Don't you have any other clothes?" That was when Ravi realized that people pay attention to clothes.

The rejection hit him hard. He lost Brinda for one and only one reason: money. The money from his position at the bowling alley. and from the housekeeping work his aging mother did, barely paid their rent and food. New clothes were a luxury he could not afford.

He learned a hard lesson that day: you may want the moon, but that does not mean the moon wants you too.

Ravi stopped eating, he lost weight, and his mother caught him staring at nothing for hours on end. He took the heartbreak hard and was convinced he would never recover. As he watched the girl of his dreams later marry a successful bureaucrat from Indian Railways, he drowned himself in work and study, scoring exceptionally in all competitive exams. His efforts ultimately got him into medical school (with the government agreeing to pay his medical-school fees for him). He was still determined to become someone worthy of Brinda.

Recently, we celebrated Ravi's new Lamborghini. It was, of course, a blue one, and after hearing his story, I was not surprised. During our conversation, Ravi wondered what Brinda would have thought about this car. I felt so sorry for my friend that day. Today, he is immensely wealthy and can date practically any woman he wants to, but it's clear that, deep in his heart, he still longs for Brinda.

I asked him what would have happened if he had married her. He said, "While I longed for her, I turned into a multimillionaire. If I had her, I would have conquered the world."

The thing is, had Brinda not left Ravi, I'm not sure he would have become who he is today. I believe he is what he is today precisely because she did not choose him. Ravi channeled the energy of unrequited love and heartbreak to transmute success. In a way, Brinda's rejection is Ravi's why.

## MERVIN'S WHY: BHARATI'S VISION OF A PERFECT WORLD

Mervin is a very successful hospitalist, with a multimillion-dollar net worth. He created his wealth mostly from his professional income and investments in healthcare startups and real estate. He also arrived in the United State as an immigrant, and I often wondered how he made it.

I still remember the first time I met him. It was at a rural hospital in northern Minnesota. I was typing a patient note on a MedSurg computer. I heard someone whistling to a famous Indian love song. He must really enjoy coming to work, I thought.

When he wasn't working, you could find Mervin driving his Porsche, often peeling corners at top speed, or at popular night clubs in the twin cities, dancing with women he met on dating apps. Most often, he was drunk.

As he swaggered through the door that day, spinning his Porsche keys in his hands, I wondered if he was even a real doctor. But then I witnessed him throw in three central lines, intubate five patients and manage an entire ICU. He was a rock star and an asset to the corporation Masood owned.

At the campfire, under the stars, Mervin stopped sipping his beer after listening to Masood and Ravi. He was quiet and reflective. I couldn't remember him ever looking like this. Mervin was a vivacious character, free-spirited, who had quite a fan following among the female nurses. He would boast about his exploits and party whenever he could. I once travelled with him in his Porsche and, given how recklessly fast he drove, I was convinced we'd die by hitting a deer or by spinning out of control, into a ditch where we would be eaten by bears or wolves.

"You know, I never wanted to become a doctor," Mervin said quietly. This caught my attention. "My father thought it would be cool to have his son's name followed by an 'MD.' My life in India was very comfortable. I had two maids who would attend to me, two cars that my father owned, and my own personal driver. I had a perfectly luxurious life. I had no ambition to do anything greater in life. My life was near perfect."

Ravi asked, "How did you end up in the United States?"

With a quick gulp of his beer, Mervin said, "It's a long story and one terrible tragedy that I wish I could go back in time and change. Time always moves forward; you cannot see what's coming, and you can't change the past. You know, I was never a party animal. My family is very conservative. I was a God-fearing Catholic and a regular churchgoer. I don't know who I am now." He shot us a sad smile.

Mervin continued, "I was forced into medical school by my dad, and I was OK with it. After all, it's cool to be a doctor, I thought. It turned out that sitting through long hours of classes and reading huge medical books was an impossible task for me. I was frustrated and ready to give up the idea of becoming a doctor."

"But you are one hell of a hospitalist. Your skills surpass most intensivists!" Masood said.

"That's now. But back then it was a different story. One day during a viva I was grilled by my physiology professor, just like a freshly caught walleye. I walked out of the examination with tears in my eyes. I'd failed." We were stunned. We couldn't imagine Mervin failing anything.

"But standing outside the exam hall with tears in my eyes was the best thing that happened to me. An angel of God came to me, wearing a yellow dress, and asked me if I was okay and if I needed help...my angel, Bharati, the most special person in my life, my best friend and the love of my life."

I thought to myself, Mervin went from a God-fearing, conservative, practicing Christian to a party monster. How could such a thing happen? I was sure Ravi and Masood also wondered the same. Who was Mervin's angel, anyway?

To Mervin, Bharati was the perfect creation of God, and the wisest of his entire batch.

The day Mervin failed his viva, Bharati sat with him and listened to him patiently, offering advice with wisdom well beyond her years. She asked how she could help him, and Mervin was speechless. No one had ever offered to help him. He asked that she help him with physiology; thus began a beautiful friendship.

Bharati is the one who taught Mervin medicine. In the classroom, the words of his professors flew over his head, but Bharati would explain the same concepts in simple words. With Bharati by his side, medicine made sense.

Not only did Mervin successfully pass his first year, he fell in love with Bharati. But he hid his emotions and focused on his studies.

As more time passed, they became close friends. They would read medical topics together, attend classes together, and have lunch and coffee together.

Bharati began opening up to him about her own story and struggles.

She was raised by a tribal farming family in a tiny village in the state of Rajasthan. Ill treatment of women was still prevalent. Honor killings were common, and the birth of a female child was considered bad luck. Bharati's father was even advised, by the village elders, to bury the newborn alive. But he was a wise, strong man and decided not to participate in this tradition of cowards. Bharati was the first person to complete college and go to medical school from her entire village. She was an inspiration and motivation to many kids.

In order to attend high school, she would walk from her village to a nearby village, in blazing desert heat. On several occasions, she was forced to quit school and college, but she always went back and persisted, against all odds. The scar on her head was from when her cousin hit her with a shovel because she refused to work on the farm, and because she used up too much oil at night reading books—they had no electricity.

Mervin's perspective on life changed after he met Bharati, and as time went by, his respect for her grew even more. During the second year of medical school, each medical student was posted in a different rural location.

The two months away from Bharati tore him apart; he missed her immensely and wondered if she felt the same for him. He continued to hide how he felt about her; even if he wanted to tell her, he couldn't simply call. Those were the early cell phone days; not everyone had one.

There was a temple on a hill nearby, and every evening, people would gather around the temple and socialize. But Mervin would sit on the stairway, up the hill that led to the temple, and gaze at the sky. It was always clear, free of light pollution, away from the city's busy life. He'd sit and stare at the stars, wondering if Bharati was doing the same.

When the two months ended, he hurried back to medical school and searched for Bharati, "running around like a mad man," in his words. There was a park, between the hospital and the medical college, where medical students usually studied. He was perspiring in the summer heat, from all the running, and needed some water and shade to cool down. When he approached a water fountain, he saw Bharati staring at him with tear-filled eyes. She ran toward him, and they embraced, the tightest of hugs. Neither spoke, but they didn't need to.

Their bond only grew with time, and Mervin discovered what his true purpose was, one day, when Bharati asked him, "What's your biggest dream?"

The question threw him off guard, and he really had to think. His life was already so comfortable. There never was an occasion when he needed something that his father could not afford. And he was with Bharati.

"I suppose becoming a doctor and making my father proud?" Bharati looked at him, her face blank and her eyes unblinking.

It was clear to him she was looking for something more profound. And that's when it hit him, what his true dream was.

"My biggest dream is the fulfillment of your dreams," He told her. "Your dreams are my dreams now."

Bharati's biggest dream wasn't just a dream, it was more like a vision of an ideal world.

She imagined a world in which no child went to bed hungry and no human was denied medical care or education, irrespective of their financial state; a world that honored human innovative skill and human progress; a system that awards human endeavors and human spirit of innovation for the betterment of all humanity; a system that ends atrocities against women and children in India and all over the world; one that honors an individual's pursuit toward their own happiness, free of discrimination and with equal opportunity.

Mervin had made notes about Bharati's vision, when she shared it with him, and would refer to them for inspiration. This is how he claims he cleared medicine. Bharati's vision of a perfect world was his why. They didn't know how they would achieve this seemingly impossible vision, but they would try, together.

Together they decided to take the USMLE (United States Medical Licensing Exam) to pursue residency in the United States. They planned to funnel their earnings into investments, like real estate, until they could achieve financial freedom. While they did so, they would continue to perform charitable medical care in India and contribute to charitable organizations that feed the hungry, and the ones that focus on women and child welfare and health. They even planned to run for Congress or the Senate and create laws that would lead to a better world, once they'd immigrated to the United States.

Mervin was determined that, with or without him, and no matter what, Bharati would become a congresswoman or senator someday.

The pair completed their final years, with excellent scores, and started their internship together. During the internship, Mervin expressed to his parents his intention to marry Bharati. But his parents did not agree. They were Catholics and she was a Hindu. His father made it clear that they would not welcome a Hindu into the family.

But that was just verbal resistance. Bharati faced a greater threat. She had to explain to her family that she loved a Christian boy and was scared to death her brothers would kill her. In her tribe in Rajasthan, women were forbidden from marrying a man outside their tribe (even a Hindu man from a different tribe was still forbidden). If it was a Muslim, Christian, or a non-Hindu, it was the end of the story for the girl and the boy who had fallen in love. It was common practice for both the boy and the girl to be killed, and such practices still happen often in rural India (this practice of killing lovers is called honor killing).

With a great deal of hesitation, Bharati said to her brother, "*Bhaiya ek ladka hai*...(Brother, there is a boy...)." But her brother did not wait for her to finish. He simply slapped her and locked her up in a room.

Luckily, Bharati managed to escape. Mervin and Bharati caught a train to Bangalore (a city in south India) and married each other in a court of law.

Bharati's family searched for them for several months. But before Bharati's family could show up at their doorstep, Mervin convinced his father to transfer a significant amount of money to him so he and Bharati could travel to the United States for the USMLE.

Before they boarded the flight to the United States, Mervin called his father, to inform him about the marriage, and asked for his blessing. He also warned his father that Bharati's family might show up at his door. It turns out her family had already shown up in search of Bharati, and his father was deeply ashamed of Mervin for marrying—against his father's will, out of his faith—a woman from a different culture and a lower class.

Bharati's family sent her a message: "Never come back or show your face again." As sad as this may all sound, they were just glad that they were still alive, not hanging from a tree as an honor killing example. Their only choice was to leave India for a better life. Mervin suspected his parents would have eventually been okay with their marriage, but Bharati was very sure her dad would have killed her had she gone back.

Once they reached the United States, they rented a friend's house in Chicago. This friend was a successful landlord and owned multiple properties in the Chicago area. They cleared their CS (clinical skills/second part of USMLE) exams and started applying for residency programs. Mervin would call India, and his mother would pick up the phone, but his dad refused to talk to him.

Theirs was a passionate love, deserving of the respect of the entire world. But it came to a tragic end.

Early one morning, while returning home from a busy night call during her second year of residency, Bharati's car spun out of control on black ice, and she was hit by a truck on a freeway. Bharati was declared dead on arrival at the ER. Mervin's entire life changed in a moment.

Mervin went into depression and drowned himself in alcohol and drugs. He cursed himself and believed he had failed Bharati. He went in search of death, but it kept evading him. One night he tried to drink himself to death and took some benzodiazepines, to ensure it would be painless, only to wake up in a hospital ICU, intubated, with a resident searching for his internal jugular with a huge needle and insufficient local anesthetic.

The creator had to be kind, he thought; every time he tried to die, he was kept alive. Every time he searched for mercy, The Creator made him taste pain. This self-torture continued for several months, with innovative different methods and different means. He even attempted to jump off a cliff in Yellowstone, hoping not to be found. Before he could jump, he saw a grizzly bear tearing through a cactus down the river. That made him decide against jumping, but he felt like a coward. And he felt his life was worthless now, without Bharati.

He later figured The Creator must be keeping him alive for a reason. Today he works hard to fulfill those dreams of Bharati's that live on in him. Bharati's vision is his life's purpose.

## YOUR WHY

Ravi somehow channeled the pain of his heartbreak, and transmuted success. Masood and Mervin somehow channeled grief, and transmuted success. It seems as if intense pain or emotion is a key to unlocking a person's true purpose. It opens them up to hear the Creator's Whisper.

All along we may have been looking at success through an incorrect lens. Rather than striving to be successful, we should be striving to find meaning in life and fulfill our purpose. To do that, we have to tune in to the whisper and find our whys. Take a look at people with fame and money or success in our world. Did they start out with the sole intention of becoming rich and famous? Or did they land there as a side effect? They are now rich and famous because they persisted toward a goal that was their true emotional calling. Often, that true calling comes out of an emotional upheaval. The fame and money are visible to the world, but successful people don't really talk about their aching hearts or a longing to change a moment in the past, unless someone sits down with them, with a cup of coffee, and asks the right questions.

Now it's time to identify your why.

Look deep inside your soul, and search your life. There may have been adversity, a great love story, a big blunder, a heartbreak, a person who believed in you, a feeling of not being wanted, or a devastating failure that turned your world upside down. It's the one thing you wish you could change, that one thing that, even to this day, fills your eyes with tears, that one thing for which you would willingly kneel at God's doorstep, even for centuries, if need be, just to turn back time.

Find that one thing, go back in time, mentally, and allow yourself to feel that emotion. You will draw inspiration and strength from it in times of hardship. When you feel like giving up, it will keep you going.

*If you can't fly then run, if you can't run then walk, if you can't walk then crawl, but whatever you do, you have to keep moving forward. (Martin Luther King Jr.)*

You might ask, "How do I even crawl when my entire world is coming to an end?" The right question to ask is not *how* but *why*. Why would you want to still crawl? What is it that you want to see changed? Why would you still crawl? You need to search your soul. The answer to that question is your why.

Without your *why* to draw strength from, you will give up. Without your *why*, you will continue to live someone else's life.

*Don't waste your time living someone else's life. (Steve Jobs)*

Every single day, when you wake up, remember that your creator is not done with you, that your purpose in life is yet to be fulfilled. If he was through with you, you would not have woken up this morning. Every person on this planet is created for a purpose, and the beneficiary of that fulfilled purpose will be the entire world.

Your pain is real; don't hide it. Embrace it. This is who you are. Acknowledge that you are human and that no one is perfect.

## HOW TO FIND YOUR WHY

Nothing worthwhile was created on this planet without human imagination.

Imagine the Creator's Whisper to be a spark, and your imagination is the fuel this spark needs so it can turn into a wildfire.

For you to find your why, I need your help and your imagination. The Creator has been whispering "your why" all along. It's time for you to tune out the worldly noise.

Let's start by asking a simple question: what will make your life slightly better tomorrow?

If you are sitting there, reading this book and thinking about figuring out how to make your rent payment tomorrow, then let's use some imagination.

Let's initiate an imaginary dialogue with a genie, like the one in Aladdin's Lamp.

This time there are no limitations on the number of wishes you can make.

He asks, "How can I make your life slightly better?" You ask him to pay your rent for the next month, and he does.

He asks again, "How can I make your life slightly better?" You ask for a million dollars, and the genie gives it to you. He asks the question again and again, and you ask for $5 million, a successful multibillion-dollar company, and for your family and friends to be rich and successful. He grants all of these wishes. When he asks the question again, you wish to become the richest, happiest, and the most successful, famous person on this planet, and so you do.

You have no more wishes, but the genie doesn't stop. "What next?" he asks.

Now that you have run out of things to wish for, let me ask you this: what is that one thing you would want to do for the betterment of all humanity?

What is that one thing you want to change for the betterment of this world, if you were not limited by the resources you possess?

What is it? What is that one thing?

Use your imagination to the fullest.

The vision your mind receives is The Creator's Whisper in your mind, your Life's Purpose.

## TRANSMUTING YOUR LIFE'S ADVERSITY INTO YOUR LIFE'S PURPOSE

Tune out that worldly noise, so you can focus on that one thought—your true purpose, the Creator's Whisper.

I believe that our creator communicates with all of us; after all, he created us for a purpose.

Some have heard this whisper and acted on it, and some just decided to hear the worldly noise.

But if you really stopped for a moment and meditated, preferably in isolation, and followed the "what next" imaginary pathway outlined above, then you will find meaning and a worthy goal to persist toward for the betterment of all creation.

Follow this whisper with all your heart.

The Creator does not do something without reason. There is a reason you picked up this book. Hear his whisper, and most importantly, recognize what it is and where it comes from, so you can change the world.

Now imagine that greatest dream being fulfilled as you read.

Do you feel the excitement? Hold that excitement in your mind.

Feel your vision coming true. Imagine yourself creating that change, and feel that satisfaction of seeing all creation better off because of you.

Deep inside your heart, you always knew it. This is truly what you always wanted to do.

The next step is difficult. You need to bring your mind to the greatest adversity you faced in your life. As you feel this excitement of a fulfilled life's purpose, mentally go back to the moment you felt the greatest pain or emotional upheaval. Imagine how you would have turned it around if there were no limitations, financial or otherwise.

Would you like to change that moment of pain, somehow, if you could?

If you answered yes, well, my friend, you know we cannot turn back time, yet!

But how would you like to save other people from the same agony, pain, or adversity?

Let's try to feel the pain of your greatest loss, and try feeling the Creator's Whisper at the same time.

These are two emotions that contradict each other.

Your mind will choose one over the other. This task is not easy.

But with time and practice, you will be able to hold the Creator's Whisper and the pain from your greatest adversity or emotional upheaval, in your mind, at the same time.

How will you know?

Initially, your mind will lean to one side (greatest adversity), with tears flowing out of your eyes. Then, momentarily, as your purpose in life is clear in your mind, you'll sway to the other side (your greatest dream), euphoria.

Your mind will sway from sadness to purpose, until it finds a happy medium somewhere in the middle (the spot in between your greatest sadness and euphoria), to the extent that, when you think of either your adversity or your purpose in life, your emotional response will become one and the same.

Why is it important to hold both conflicting emotions in your mind at the same time?

There is a strong neurochemical circuit of neurons (nerve cells) in your brain. It stores the memory of your greatest loss and the emotional upheaval that followed it.

When you bring this moment of loss back into your mind, you will still feel that pain. If you do still feel the pain, this means this neural circuit is still a gold mine of unlimited emotional energy.

By doing the above exercise of holding two emotions of opposite natures in your mind, at one time, you incorporate your life's purpose (your Creator's Whisper) into the same memory pathway/neural circuit that stores your greatest emotional pain.

Hence, every time you feel your greatest emotional pain, you will activate the pathway to your purpose in life. You not only have found your why, but you've also learned to transmute your greatest loss into a meaningful purpose.

This is how you persist, in the face of all challenges, toward your goal. You transmute your emotional energy from your greatest loss into your greatest purpose in life.

# Chapter 2

# SEXUAL ENERGY

"Let me tell you something about lions..." Ravi began, after a heavy swig from his coffee mug.

Masood looked at Mervin and me and said, "Did the sun rise from the west? For this man to not talk about stocks today."

Mervin laughed. "I should watch the sunrise tomorrow; maybe it *will* rise from the west."

Masood had a point. Ravi not talking about investments was rare indeed. Ravi simply smiled, eyes sparkling.

"When a lion challenges another dominant lion, to take control of the pride, the challenging lion risks losing his life. Do you know why he is risking his life?" Ravi asked.

I didn't quite know the answer, so I chose to remain quiet. After all, who among us would have studied lions? We were medical doctors, and so was Ravi. Why the interest in leonine behavior?

Ravi answered his own question. "The challenging lion is willing to risk his life for one thing and one thing only: sex!"

Well, that made sense. He had captured my attention, and from the looks of it, Mervin's and Masood's as well. Maybe Ravi was about to talk about all his sexual escapades. I was sure he must have met many wonderful women on dating apps, and I hoped he'd describe these meetups in detail. I thought: this will be fun.

I got ahead of myself and asked Ravi, "Where did you meet them? Which is the best dating app?"

Ravi ignored me and said, "If you've been looking for the most powerful force on the planet, which can help you become profoundly successful, you may find what I am about to say very interesting and unusual at the same time."

What could be more unusual than Masood's Creator's Whisper?

"Are you kidding me?" Masood asked. "You had our full attention the moment you uttered the word sex."

"When I say the word sex, I don't just mean the mere biological act," Ravi said. "It has a far deeper meaning. There are many books that talk about sexual energy, but no one really teaches you how to harness it for success."

Mervin sat expressionless, staring at Ravi. His eyes were wide open, and I'm pretty sure his pupils were dilated with excitement. I'm also pretty sure I had exactly the same expression.

"Your gender does not matter," Ravi explained. "You can summon this energy and harness it irrespective of your sexual orientation. If you are good-looking and have a hot date waiting for you, every night, on a dating site, and all you do is show up, chat a little, and take him or her to bed with you, you have it all wrong. It may very well be that you have been squandering away your precious sexual energy for pennies."

I began to think that I should have held my horses and not assumed that we'd be getting fun details of Ravi's sex life.

"Ravi, what exactly are you saying? Are you suggesting people stop enjoying sex?" Masood asked.

"I am not against enjoying sex," Ravi clarified. "I'm saying that sex with a person who helps you harness this massive force—sexual energy—may increase the odds of you achieving the things you may want to achieve."

"Harnessing sexual energy" was a weird concept, one that I had vaguely heard about, but I had never met anyone who actually harnessed it, until now.

"I am not the best-looking guy," Ravi continued. "So I have had to work really hard for sex. This is why I've researched this topic extensively. Once someone has harnessed their sexual energy, they can transmute success and become wealthy."

But I wondered: is it possible to somehow combine sex and productivity in order to become successful?

Ravi said he would conquer the world if Brinda was on his side. Is this what he meant?

## DON'T NOT HAVE SEX

Before I share Ravi's secret to harnessing sexual energy, let's talk about how *not* to harness it. You cannot attain sexual transmutation by avoiding sex, no matter what YouTube pundits preach. You have probably heard anti-sex rhetoric like "Don't have sex!" and "Stop masturbating!"

If you followed the teachings of these so-called pundits, you would be so sexually frustrated that, by the time you completed their suggested tasks, you would "be ready to hump a cow walking down the streets in India," in Ravi's words.

Not having sex means you only crave it more. And so avoiding masturbation is not the answer. It's unhealthy not to masturbate, and it's unnatural to not have or enjoy sex. Social Media pundits have no idea what they're talking about, as they don't understand how sexual energy works or how to actually harness it.

## WHY WE HAVE SEX: THE ORGASM

To understand sexual transmutation, you must ask: why do we have sex? The generic answer is, of course, that the act of sex is fun and that there is nothing more satisfying than an orgasm.

In biological terms, the act of sex leads to the secretion of the hormone called oxytocin. This leads to a rhythmic muscle contraction of the genital muscles, followed by ejaculation of genital secretions. This release of oxytocin causes an orgasm, and generally, the larger the oxytocin amount, the larger the orgasm. After that, the nucleus acumens in our brain reward us with a good amount of dopamine, which gives us relaxing pleasure. After we experience this, we continue to crave more of it.

Granted, I may have taken the fun out of sex for you by describing it as simply the act of rubbing your genitals to bring about the release of certain chemicals in our brains, not unlike the way Marcus Aurelius did, years ago, by writing: "As for sexual intercourse, it is the friction of a piece of gut and, following a sort of convulsion, the expulsion of some mucus." (I bet Marcus Aurelius lost his fan following after he made this statement.) But the point is that nature has somehow tricked us into rubbing our genitals repeatedly, while all the fun happens inside our brains.

## FIND WHAT MAKES YOUR BRAIN ORGASM

Sex isn't the only activity that leads to the release of positive neurochemicals in your brain, giving someone the same satisfaction as an orgasm. The key to sexual transmutation is finding the activity that works for you.

Ravi approached a number of people who seemed stuck in their fields and posed the question, "Is there anything in your life that gives you satisfaction the way a good orgasm does?" Most of them said nothing could beat an orgasm.

But when Ravi approached a bunch of people who were highly successful in their fields and asked each of them what gave them the same satisfaction as an orgasm, he got a different type of response. A successful bariatric surgeon said, "A perfectly executed surgery." Every time he put on his surgical gown and walked into the operation theatre, he chased that high. An exceptional basketball player felt orgasmic every time the ball swooshed through the basket. An award-winning sprinter said she felt that way every time she came first in a 100-meter dash.

The day you experience the same satisfaction as an orgasm, if not more, from a productive, nonsexual act, is the day you have successfully transmuted sexual energy into something that will make you very successful. This does not mean you need to give up the enjoyment of sexual acts with your partner. You can enjoy both, the satisfaction of orgasm with your partner and the satisfaction from the transmuted productive act.

The stronger your urge for sex, and the higher your appetite for the act of sex, the stronger your affection toward your transmuted act will be, and both result in greater satisfaction.

But I should caution you, if you just enjoy sex because you have a very strong urge for it, and for the sake of your satisfaction, it will take you on a nonproductive and disastrous path. Sexual energy is a very powerful force. The inability to harness this power, and your unwillingness to productively channel it, could lead to devastation.

There are many stories of very prominent people unable to successfully transmute sexual energy, and they continue to seek satisfaction through sexual orgasm. Because of this, they ruined their reputation. This is similar to people, in younger age groups, who lack the will to appropriately channel this energy. They keep moving, from partner to partner, chasing the release of these chemicals in their brain, in search of more. Such individuals will not perform anything worthwhile in their lives, until they have somehow learned to channel this energy and transmute it into something productive that will eventually make them very successful and wealthy. This is one of the strongest reasons why you will find more people achieving success in older ages than in their teen years. Of course, there are exceptions.

## SEX ADDICTION

Ask an alcoholic what gives him satisfaction equivalent to orgasm. He will say a sip of alcohol. Ask a drug addict what gives him satisfaction equivalent to orgasm. He will say drugs. A person who has sex for the sake of sex and the satisfaction of the orgasm seeks out more sex. They are chasing after the release of these chemicals, without putting it into a good transmutable purpose— they are chasing sex just for sex. They will not achieve anything worthwhile, just like an alcoholic or a drug addict. In simple words, they are just sex addicts.

The cure to sex addiction is sexual transmutation. I am sure other addictions can be studied and found to have similar cures.

It's important to note the comparison between two orgasms experienced by a single person who indulges in a sexual act, one with a person they love intensely, and another with a person they simply feel attracted to.

The difference is vast. If we consider sex on a scale of one hundred, then an orgasm with the partner we love intensely would be 10,000/100, and an orgasm with a partner we find attractive but do not love, would be more like 50–70/100.

Note: finding a soulmate not only compounds sexual satisfaction but also compounds success, when transmuted.

## HOW TO TRANSMUTE SEXUAL
## ENERGY FOR SUCCESS

Sexual energy can be transmuted, from anyone to whom you are sexually attracted, into any productive act you set your mind to. Yes, *anything* you set your mind to. If you have already found an activity that gives you the same satisfaction as an orgasm, that's great! But if you are as yet to find one, I will teach you how.

I have done the heavy weightlifting and the hard work for you. Are you ready? At first you may not believe me. But I want you to trust me. Physiologically speaking, I intend to teach you how to hijack the sexual-satisfaction, neurochemical circuit that already exists in your brain.

When nature created you and me, it decided to place a default pathway in our brains that creates satisfaction from having sex. Why? Because it was nature's way to ensure we kept reproducing so humanity, or for that matter any creature, would not go extinct.

So how then do you hijack this default pathway to ensure a similar satisfaction be created from a nonsexual act?

Transmutation, precisely through the art of transmutation.

Recall how Masood would sit under the streetlamp studying, solving math or physics problems. He would close his eyes and imagine himself wearing scrubs or a surgical gown. He would imagine that his patient was treated very well. He imagined himself saving someone's life, the pride in his parents' eyes and the gratitude of his patient's relatives. He just imagined it all in detail, in great detail. He started falling in love with his imagination and his own imaginary world, which he had created in isolation, under a streetlamp, while studying. As he got older his mind wandered, and temptations, like partying and dating girls, threatened his focus. But he did not give in. He tricked his mind and cut out the person to whom he was most sexually attracted and pasted the vision of himself as a physician. He replaced things that would lead him astray, with his imagined vision.

And this is exactly what you need to do. It will not be easy, and it will, no doubt, require a lot of practice. However, this is the first step in the direction of sexual transmutation.

At first it will be hard, because the sexual circuit in our brain has evolved, over generations, to ensure we reproduce. To replace the image of reproductive genitalia, or a vision of a body part that gets you sexually aroused, with a nonsexual goal you intend to achieve, is not an easy task.

Masood replaced the image of a hot, sexy woman with the visions of wearing a white coat or scrubs and imagined himself as a successful doctor, and then masturbated to it.

Similarly, you could replace anything and everything that sexually arouses you with a productive act that is a part of your goal and dream. You may also want to masturbate while doing so. For example, if you hate math or have difficulty with math, start by thinking that math is sexy.

If you think this sounds perverted, I want you to pause, for a moment, and just hear me out until the end of this section. As odd as it may sound, this is a purposeful perversion, created to penetrate your brain's sexual neural circuit.

First of all, it's not easy, let me remind you. It's not easy to masturbate imagining the house of your dreams, the apartment complex you intend to buy, or a career you want to embrace. It will take practice to overwrite the sexual pathway/neural circuit in your brain so that, in the future, not only will you have a thought of the hot, other person who excites you, but also your vision of success. Both will generate similar sexual excitement. Think of your future mansion as you masturbate; the more you practice, the better it gets.

What then is the result? Do you remember the euphoria you felt when you made love for the first time with a person you truly cared about? You will feel the same euphoria when you think of your career, business, dream home, or investments. That euphoria will result in you persisting toward your desired goal. All I am trying to do is replace that sexy person of your dreams with a career, business, or your dream home inside the brain's sexual neural circuit.

Many of us have done it, and I want to say that it's not impossible.

When you succeed, you will turn into the lion who is willing to risk its life for success. In this case, it's your transmuted act for sex. You would have harnessed the energy from the pathway of the sexual circuit in your brain for an act that is not sexual. In a true sense, you have tapped into your sexual energy and unleashed one of the greatest secrets to success.

The euphoria of chasing success will now be akin to enjoying a sexual act with an intensely desired partner.

## SEXUAL ENERGY ISN'T FINITE

Now, you may be wondering, if I transmute all my sexual energy, will I lose my sexual urge toward my partner?

Absolutely not. In fact, it's the opposite. As you become more successful, your urge to indulge in sexual activity with your partner compounds, and vice versa. This continues to give you greater and greater satisfaction in life. Essentially, you have now hijacked the same neurochemical pathway for two activities.

Through sexual transmutation, both the act of sex and the act of success resulted in the utilization of the same brain neural circuit that resulted in the release of similar neurochemicals, which led to the satisfaction equivalent of an orgasm.

Perhaps you may have more than one nonsexual activity to recruit into your brain's sexual circuit, and you're wondering if this is possible. Yes, it absolutely is possible. The number of activities you can add has no limits, at least according to what we know now.

## INCORPORATING A PARTNER (OR SOULMATE) INTO THE SEXUAL CIRCUIT

Many of us who understand the chemistry and the unique nature of our brains have learned to tap into it, knowingly, while some have done so without help, or unknowingly.

Recall that sexual transmutation of energy, from a partner you love into a productive act, is far more profound and powerful than a mere act of sexual transmutation that does not involve love. Why is sexual satisfaction with a person you love so profoundly satisfying? It is precisely because that person you love has unconsciously hijacked the sexual pathway in your brain already. Every time you interact or indulge in sexual activity with them, you activate this pathway, resulting in greater and greater satisfaction.

By now you know that, by imagining the acts of success and creating sexual arousal toward them, you can learn to incorporate them into your sexual circuit.

The reverse is also true: having sex with a soulmate who has already been transcribed into this sexual circuit leads to activation of this circuit. The more it's activated, the stronger it gets, through the release of more and more neurochemicals.

Transmuting a nonsexual act into this strengthened sexual circuit increases the probability of success and, possibly, compounds the degree of success, compared to a nonsexual act transmuted through a sexual circuit alone (without love from a soulmate).

You may be wondering, How do I find such a partner to incorporate into my sexual circuit?

It is important to point out that there are three types of mating partners.

1. Soulmate (your neurochemical and biological pathways are preprogrammed to make this determination)
2. Practical mate (determined by the conscious part of your brain)
3. So-so mate (other sexual partners, who do not bring about a huge neurochemical bump in the sexual circuit, the ones that do not belong to either 1 or 2)

Here's how to find a practical mate, who may or may not be your soulmate.

(Note: if a person turns out to be both your soul and practical mate, you are one of the very blessed!)

Write down your conscious criteria of what you want and, more importantly, what you don't want in a partner. Remember that what you *don't* want is often the reason you get divorced or separated.

As important as it may be to look for qualities you want, it is more important to outline, in detail, what you don't want in your partner for a long-lasting, fruitful relationship.

You see, one of the greatest hindrances to building wealth is a bad marriage or an ugly divorce.

Take a sheet of paper, make two columns, and write down the qualities and characteristics, in an ascending or descending order, from most liked to least liked and most disliked to least disliked. This is your search criteria.

Then go search, and also have other people, or search engines, search for you. This process helps build clarity in your mind to look for a practical partner who will work for you and has the least likelihood of your relationship ending in separation or ending up with a broken family.

If intelligence is a criteria for you, write it down. Also write down what aspect of intelligence you desire and how you intend to grade it.

Once you have found such a match, the next step is to align this matched person with the unconscious algorithm in your brain, based on chemical interactions, emotions, and intuition.

This process happens with time. In layperson terms, you will call this "the act of falling in love."

Finding a soulmate is the second step, not the first.

You let your conscious mind determine the practical mate. This process has been achieved by the checklist criteria enlisted above by your conscious mind.

Now allow this consciously selected person to be tested against the unconscious part of your mind. The unconscious part of your mind has the neurochemical, emotional, and intuitional makeup to determine the best genetic and satisfactory sexual fit for you. It's the one who most aligns with the sexual circuit in your brain and who has a high probability of enhancing the sexual circuit in your brain.

Most often, we allow our unconscious brain to make the soul-mate-finding decision before the filtration process. Then we fall madly in love with a person who doesn't fit the practical-mate criteria. Separations often happen from the conscious part of the mind, and it will usually be a result of the things we dislike. Separating a soulmate from a strong neurochemical circuit is a devastating process when practical aspects don't align.

But if we found all practical mates and then tested them against our soul-mate-finding algorithm in our brain, there is a possibility we could all be more satisfied, happier, and able to transmute greater success by using the strengthened sexual pathway, through the love of a soulmate who is also a good practical fit.

Disclaimer: the author takes no responsibility for any sexual or behavioral issues that may or may not result from the practice of concepts listed in this book. The author by no means is trying to influence your decisions. The only purpose of this book is to educate and point out aspects of lives of some successful people. Concepts in this book are some of the means but are not the only means of transmuting success.

# Chapter 3

# INVESTING IN THE STOCK MARKET

"Ravi, what gives you nonsexual satisfaction, equivalent to an orgasm?" I asked, warming my hands by the campfire, head still swimming with what I'd learned about sexual transmutation.

Ravi took a sip of his coffee, and with a twinkle in his eye, he replied, "Every time my investments make money and every time I seek out and initiate an investment in a profitable venture."

I wasn't surprised by the answer. Ravi is the smartest investor among us. When he speaks about stocks and the approach to investments, it is as if he is Benjamin Graham reincarnated.

"Can you teach me how you invest? Could you give me some tips on what to look for, how, and what to buy?" I asked, reaching for my own cup of coffee.

Ravi smiled and said, "I don't provide stock tips. But I can teach you the right approach to investing in the stock market, which will, over time, make you very wealthy."

Never did I imagine that, on a fishing trip in northern Minnesota, I would learn the most important investing lessons in my life. Around a campfire with friends, delicious drinks in hand, I learned that what I'd been doing all along was wrong. In the sections ahead, I've laid out exactly what I learned from Ravi that night under the stars.

Disclaimer: this chapter is written to help you adopt the correct approach to investing in the stock market. This section is not intended to give you stock tips or investment advice. I am not an investment advisor. If I mention the name of a company, it does not imply that you should invest in it. This section is for educational purposes only and meant to outline various common and uncommon methods available, to help you determine the right approach.

## THE BEST AND BRIGHTEST COMPANIES

One of the greatest blessings of our generation is the opportunity to invest and buy some of the most successful companies in the world. On a computer or a smartphone, with a simple click of a button, you can become the owner of some of the most outstanding companies on the planet, companies like Apple, Amazon, Microsoft, Facebook, Tesla, Walmart, Google, etc.

It is important to note that, technically, nothing is stopping anyone from saving some money and buying a stock of a good company, or a bunch of companies, through an ETF (Electronically Traded Fund) or mutual fund. Your choice of wanting or not wanting to own is completely independent of others' opinions. You may choose to own corporate America (American company stocks), and all the human ingenuity and innovation in it, or not choose to own it. The choice is yours, but if you choose not to own some, then no one is to blame. I have met some people who have a six-figure salary but choose to spend it all on nice luxuries and liabilities (things you buy that cost you more money to keep or use and enjoy) and complain that the 1 percent has ripped off the entire planet.

The point is you may choose to own the spirit of human innovation (the human ability to invent something new, which becomes valuable) within Corporate America or choose not to own it.

What exactly is this "spirit of human innovation?" Entrepreneurship. More specifically, it is the fire that ignites in the heart of every person in the pursuit of their American dream. It is the blueprint of success that is born in the heart of every soul who has set foot on this promised land while in pursuit of their American dream. The spirit of human innovation is the very fabric of our nation. It resides in every heart that intends to change this world for the better.

There is a massive number of entrepreneurs out there and many millions more who dream about becoming entrepreneurs. I am an entrepreneur myself and dream of starting more companies in the future.

A company is essentially nothing but a collection of people putting together their ideas and ingenuity to solve a human problem, create goods and services to solve a problem, or make human life better.

However, mathematically speaking, only 25–30 percent of them will go from an idea stage to raising a series A funding round (meaning their company is worthy of investor money). Among those, only about half receive a series B funding (meaning they're worthy of more investor money), and then only half or so of those receive a series C, and that number continues to halve with every additional step. Then the very small number of companies that have survived go public (meaning they get listed on the stock exchange), and very, very few of those leave a legacy big enough to become a household name.

What I am trying to say is that most companies fail before they ever go public. But the ones that do go public get listed on the stock exchange and tend to have a strong spirit of human innovation backing them.

However, wouldn't it be nice to have a crystal ball of some sort and to spot a legacy company at its idea stage, before it turns huge like Apple, Google, Amazon, or Facebook, and then to buy it very early, at the idea stage or series-funding-round stages, when it is inexpensive, so then we can all become multimillionaires or, possibly, billionaires?

You may be thinking: Which company should I buy? Or which one is going to make me rich?

These aren't the right questions to ask. It's extremely difficult for a company to go from an idea stage to IPO (initial public offering/being listed on the stock market), because the chance of failure is so high.

This book is not about finding a student-Bill Gates at Harvard, to invest in early Microsoft; it's about understanding how to build long-term wealth and success without having to need a crystal ball.

Think about it for a good moment. The companies that exist on the S&P 500 Index (The S&P 500 Index, or the Standard & Poor's 500 Index, is a market-capitalization-weighted index of the 500 largest US publicly-traded companies.) have survived all the series-funding steps I outlined above. The chance of success or failure, at every step, was 50/50. Well, these companies are not lemonade stands. They are companies created by people with hard work, persistence, and ingenuity, in whose hearts resides this spirit of innovation.

## THE SPIRIT OF HUMAN INNOVATION

Ravi recalled a quote he once read: "'A person's best friend is his hindsight, because that is all that person has.'"

"Very true," Masood said. "In about thirty to forty years from now, what would the world look like? Better or worse?"

"That's a difficult question," I replied, "because I can't see the future."

Masood continued to ask, "If better, then why? And if worse, then why?"

I thought to myself and said, "Humans invented the light bulb, the steam engine, the computer. The spirit of innovation in human hearts will continue to innovate.

So with more innovation and progress, the world will be better.

That was easy. If the world is getting better, as a result of human innovation, then the ability to innovate will only become more valuable.

Let's now think of a not-so-great scenario. What if the world got worse? Then one of several scenarios could happen, and we may go extinct, in which case, it would not matter what we own.

An asteroid may hit us, or the earth may warm too much, or a solar storm may destroy everything we care about. In that case, again, there is not a whole lot that we could do.

But what if humanity innovated, like before, and found a solution to divert such asteroids heading toward the planet? Or what if humanity found a solution to global warming or, somehow, figured out how to shield the earth before a solar storm? What would be the price of such human innovation?

Regardless of the better-or-worse scenario, we can all agree that the ability of humanity to innovate is the single most valuable asset humanity has ever possessed.

Now that we have outlined the above argument, you will realize that one method of becoming successful and wealthy is to invent something that solves a human problem. Another means to similar success would be to own someone else's invention that solves a problem, or to own someone's ability to invent or solve a problem.

For example, we are amidst the COVID-19 crisis as I type this manuscript. During this pandemic, we do have a lot of things to worry about. But would you doubt the ability and the spirit of innovation that reside in all the hearts of our healthcare workers and scientists trying to create a cure or vaccine? Think again; how wonderful would it be if you owned the creative ability of such doctors and scientists.

Is there a way to do it? Yes. Absolutely.

You can own a healthcare company that is likely to come up with a vaccine, or several healthcare companies that are likely to come out with a drug or vaccine via a low-cost ETF.

Yes, my friend, you can own the spirit of innovation of a human mind that is not yours.

What would happen if a company created a drug or vaccine that every human on this planet will need?

Your ownership of such company stock would give you ownership of that company and a share of its monetary gains. What people often forget is that every invention and progress that the smart minds in these companies make also belongs to them.

And that is the secret to long-term wealth. It's not the mere ownership of a company's ticker symbol, which changes in price every second. It's the ownership of the spirit of innovation of the minds inside it.

If the spirit of human innovation is only going to become more valuable, tomorrow, would it not be prudent to buy some of those innovative minds today?

Companies are driven by the spirit of human innovation, which is the strongest and the mightiest force on this planet.

The coming together of innovative minds that solve a problem, that lead to change in human life or behavior, etc., typically for the better, which then leads to the creation of monetary value—via sales of a product or service—is called a business/a company.

There are big companies and small companies, but each one was created by one or more entrepreneurs carrying the flame of the spirit of human innovation.

This force placed a man on the moon. This force created all the technology we see. This force created all the medication that keeps us alive. This force will put humans on Mars, solve all modern problems, and make humans immortal someday.

For the world's largest and best American companies to be incapacitated and go out of business, all at once, the world would probably have to be ending, which would mean there are bigger issues to face than those of investments. As long as the world is here the world will need goods and services, and the ones providing them will be among the best and brightest American companies.

It's February 28, 2020, today, and while I write this book, during this period of a novel coronavirus outbreak, I find people are understandably scared. The Dow Jones has dropped 4,000 points today. While I write this book, I'm watching the market in a free fall.

My advice to you will be: do not panic during any such future events.

Here are some things to keep in mind and a few questions to ask yourself. Will the best and brightest minds stop inventing? Will there be less innovation following any such crisis? Will people stop buying all the necessary goods and services?

If your answer is no, maybe you should not be selling companies on the stock market, but rather buying, now, because the same spirit of innovation is now cheaper to own.

## DON'T SHORT THE MARKET

If there is one thing you want to take home after reading this book, then remember this: no matter what and no matter who tells you to, don't ever short sell corporate America or the spirit of American innovation in it.

Short selling is the act of betting against the market/stock/ETF, etc., where you make money, as the market or stock goes down in value, and you lose money if the market or stock goes up or increases in value. It is the act of selling borrowed securities (stocks, bonds, etc.).

For more details, refer to Appendix Section 1.

## MR. PUNDIT

Pundit: self-proclaimed expert.

If anyone ever tells you to steer clear from investing in the stock market, which includes the best and brightest American corporations, please ignore them.

A stock market pundit's ulterior motive is to take your money away. Do not trust so-called pundit economists, analysts projecting earnings, pundits, fund managers forecasting future prices of stocks, and money managers who claim they can outperform the market with choice.

If you are new to the stock market and all of this is too much, simply remember: you will always be better off not listening to a pundit.

A simple dollar-cost average strategy of investing will make you far wealthier than any advice from these so-called "experts."

Dollar-cost investing is a simple strategy of investing a fixed amount of money into a low-cost index fund (like an S&P 500 index fund, such as SPY and others) over a long period of time. As the market goes down, your money will buy more shares. As the market goes up, your money will buy fewer shares. With time, you own more and more shares, which increases your long-term wealth and your net worth.

Pundits and their forecasts are unreliable. Most of them make a living forecasting, and they make a living off your fear and your greed. If a pundit says you should buy a stock or sell another because it's going up or down in value, or if they tell you to borrow money up to your eyeballs because interest rates are very low, or if they claim to teach you how and when to short the market, and they claim to be an accurate predictor of a market peak just before a crash, then those pundits made their money by teaching, not by actually doing what they preached.

Masood actually encountered one such pundit, who never owned a single stock but claimed to be an expert at stock investing. This pundit was teaching people how to short and trade in the stock market, via online classes.

### SINGLE PUNDIT

There will be some pundits who will tell you, at a family gathering, how they made a 90 percent return on a "single" stock investment. But they'll never tell you how they also lost 90 percent on another single stock on a short-term trade.

They will never tell you that they were trying to get rich quick, and in their get-rich-quick scheme, they pissed away their net worth for some short-term excitement.

Buying/investing in a single stock, with all your savings (not diversifying), and hoping to become wealthy is a very risky strategy. Beware of single-stock-promoting pundits. These pundits are usually fans of a single company or a single product of a given company.

Refer to Appendix section 2: Single pundit "pump-and-dump scheme."

## GOLD BUG PUNDITS

There are "Gold Bug Pundits" out there who hoard gold/silver/ precious metal, etc., and make it their life's mission to scare people into running away from the stock market and toward gold. They do this just to drive up the price. Some pundits will instill so much fear into people about the stock market that they will go to the extent of discrediting the government and its currency, so people chase gold out of fear. Then as the price of gold goes up, they sell their gold to people who believe them. These pundits have one primary goal: their own financial well-being. Stay far away from them.

## MISINFORMATION PUNDITS

There is so much misinformation in the investment world, and there are many people who make money teaching people how to make money. Such people never made a single penny through actual investments (buying a business, etc.) or capital gain (buying and selling an investment and realizing a profit doing so).

Whenever someone says, "I am going to teach you how to make money," run away. What that person needs is to teach him/herself how to make money before teaching you. Some of these financial pundits/gurus are so broke that they need you to sign up for their financial education classes. There are some gurus out there who will convince you that your school or college education is worthless and that you must not attend college. They want you to drop out of college and then hand over your money so they can teach you how to make money. Remember, there will always be an upsell of their courses. Then they will want you to buy more of their courses, so they can make more money from you.

## MENTOR PUNDIT

Then there are those who are looking to mentor you. They will talk about how broke they were and the challenges they faced before they became a success. But they want you to pay them to share that wisdom with you. Run from such people as well. Real, successful mentors don't need your money. Successful people will teach you what they know, if they want to, irrespective of your ability to pay or what you can offer them. If you are serious and seek honest help, successful people will help you. They will have no upsell courses, and they will not need your money. Most likely, they have created the majority of their wealth through capital gains, or by creating and running successful businesses, or they have very successful professional lives.

## DROPOUT PUNDITS

Do not drop out of school or college. I hear of some of these pundits who provide you with so-called financial education. The stupidest decision a student can make is to drop out of their educational program. It is important to learn about money, investments, and personal finances, without a doubt. But it is also important to understand heavenly bodies, understand concepts in physics, learn chemistry, history, geography, biology, etc. Remember, education is about improving yourself. Do not look at any knowledge and say it's a waste. Don't be ignorant and narrow-minded and wonder why you learned trigonometry or quadratic equations when you only needed addition and subtraction to survive. It's like we humans saying all we need is air to breathe, in order to survive. How are humans different from, say, animals? Without understanding how the lungs and the blood vessels inside the lungs function, you are wasting these wonderful brains given by nature to improve humanity and innovate.

These words from Masood make so much sense today. You will only know the importance of lungs and their function when you contract a lung infection. Without the knowledge of medicine and biology, more lives would have been lost during the COVID-19 pandemic. Had every human focused on the knowledge of making money, but neglected every other knowledge, no human would live long enough to ensure the survival of humanity.

Don't confuse wealth accumulation and knowledge accumulation. Nothing is stopping you from accumulating both and becoming rich in both knowledge and wealth. Do not leave your education; do not drop out of your school or college. Learn how to learn, and then accumulate knowledge. Both are equally important. Don't ignore self-improvement and knowledge accumulation once you have accumulated wealth. It's akin to saying, "I have a heart that pumps blood to keep me alive. I don't need a brain." Do not show ignorance toward knowledge, which helps you understand nature and yourself. Accumulation of wealth alone is not success; sustained humility to learn more is. Always have the humility to learn more. Irrespective of your income or net worth, learn more.

## PUNDITS IN SUITS

"There is one more pundit, who does not have the appearance of a pundit," Ravi added. "This pundit will wear a suit and shiny shoes and will sell you something called whole life insurance."

Mervin nodded. "These insurance agents are after all doctors like leeches."

Ravi said, "I call them 'wholy-shit.' 'Wholy' stands for whole life insurance, and shit because if you buy one of them, you will be in deep shit."

Masood laughed. "Wholy-shit. I like it."

Ravi said, "I do believe everyone should buy term life insurances and invest wisely. But 'wholy-shit' is a no!"

"This pundit in a suit will convince you that it is the best-kept secret the world has yet to discover," Mervin explained. "It will feel like an angel has come to you to present the answer to your personal problems."

Now Ravi was laughing and said, "Once this 'wholy-shit' pundit starts presenting, you start realizing why you have always been so poor and have struggled all your life while the Rothschilds and the Rockefellers have continued to rule the world. These 'wholy-shit' pundits will even show you how to create your own bank. You will sit there and wonder at what a fool you have been. They will show you how to borrow money from yourself and pay interest to yourself, and you will wonder if that is even possible. You will sit there, shooting yourself in the foot, jump into one of these shenanigans, and will hand over your wealth to this pundit in a cheap suit. Then one night when you are lying in your bed, you will wonder why you are still struggling."

I thought to myself how lucky I was that such a pundit didn't get me first. Surely, I was stupid enough to have pissed away my money, making the pundit rich.

Ravi continued, "First of all, whole life insurance is not an investment; it's just very expensive life insurance, as long as you make your premium payments. What you develop, as you make premium payments, is cash value, which grows at a pathetic rate. And no, you don't pay interest to yourself. You pay interest to the insurance company."

I paused. "Why do people do that to themselves?"

Mervin replied, "Because people think they met an angel, who has a solution to all their problems."

Ravi continued, "They will offer you a choice to invest this cash value or match stock-market returns on your cash value, for a hefty fee, and will cap it (put a stop to it) at a certain percentage gain."

Masood said, "Basically, overall you would be better off just investing in a low-cost index fund with a long-term investment perspective and just buy term life insurance, which is inexpensive."

"Whole life insurance is a complex financial instrument that looks like it has been made for you," Ravi said. "But the truth is, it's not; it's made to make the company selling it more profitable. It may or may not make you wealthy or preserve wealth, depending on how it's structured. But I know for sure that it makes the insurance company very wealthy. Or why else would they even sell it?"

Wisdom: buy term life insurance and invest the rest of your savings. Do not buy whole life insurance.

## WHEN THE WORLD FEELS LIKE IT'S ENDING

As the coronavirus market correction unfolded, I thought to myself, *Some losers will do anything for some fame, publicity, and to take more money from other scared people.* If only they spent more time creating something of phenomenal value (started a company, solved a problem, cured a disease, etc.) than being fortune tellers. Some pundits claimed, on news channels, that they had predicted the COVID-19 crisis accurately, while if you look at their teachings, they have been forecasting this stock-market crash for the last ten years, while sitting on the sidelines, away from the stock market. If they really had a crystal ball, they could have multiplied their wealth many times over by now. Instead, they sat on the sidelines, missing out on one of the greatest bull markets in stock-market history. I pity the scared students of those fortune-telling pundits who have missed out on true wealth-building opportunities like these in the past.

As I write this book, I do not know if the market will go down further tomorrow.

I decided to stick with the wisdom of my wealthy friends and chose to ignore the pundits. I bought stocks, as the market went down, choosing to own the spirit of innovation at a cheaper price. I decided to adhere to Ravi's advice: if the world ends tomorrow, your cash is no good and neither is your gold or your stock. But if the world survives, it will not be because of cash, gold, or Bitcoin. It will be because of the ability of humans to innovate.

When the world is in a panic and everyone is selling a piece of the spirit of human innovation, as companies and stocks they own, what you should do is buy and own a piece of this spirit being sold at a discounted price.

When the stock market crashes and it is raining money for the common man, you need to go out there with a bucket, not a thimble.

When people think the world is ending, you must remember this wisdom of the wealthy.

Buy the best and brightest American companies with the most intense spirit of human innovation in them.

When the market is crashing or going down, do not panic; do not buy gold; do not buy bonds or phantom coins/poop coins/ Bitcoins. "Buy stocks."

## BIRDS OF A FEATHER

Birds of a feather flock together is an old saying, and one might wonder why. If you look carefully, successful people always connect with other very successful people or like-minded people. The drug addicts find solace in proving to each other why their abuse of drugs is justified. Alcoholics connect with other alcoholics and convince each other that their suffering is worth a drink. If you want to be successful, the first thing you must do is change the way you think and think like the successful do. And so, a good way to seek out real success, in investing, is to learn from people who have achieved it.

Had I not met these wealthy, self-made millionaires. I would have never learned from their wisdom. If I had continued to hang out with my drunk, weed-addicted bum friends, I would have become one of them. I would never have been able to write this book. You must choose your friends and life partners very carefully.

It's time for you to dump your useless friends. Seek out successful people, and learn from them. Seek out wealthy people, and learn from them.

Your net worth will be the average of the four to five people you hang out with.

If your friends are all multimillionaires, you will become one.

If your friends are all billionaires, you will become one.

If you hang out with broke friends, you will become one.

## WHAT IS THE STOCK MARKET?

What is the stock market? What is a stock? If you think it's a ticker symbol that is worth a little bit of money and constantly goes up and down in value, you would be wrong.

If you said, "The stock market is a place where pieces of a company (stocks) are sold and bought," you're on the right track.

My next question is, what is a company?

The explanation is slightly different from what you would find in a dictionary.

In Ravi's wise words, "The power of imagination is far superior to practical observation, but only if one acts on it."

One day, a kid at a university dreamt of a world where everyone had their own computers. One day, some kids dreamt of a virtual place where people could meet, discuss, share pictures, and store their memories. One day, two kids came up with an idea and a plan to create a search engine on the internet. One day, a person had an idea of creating a bookstore online. One man dreamt of colonizing Mars, and self-driving cars. A bunch of kids, under the imagination of a visionary, created a powerful computer that you carry, every day, in your pocket, and something you can't live without today. They worked hard on these ideas and got interested people to help, some with money, some with effort and time, and others with more ideas. When the world realized the value of change these ideas created, everyone wanted a piece of it in exchange for their wealth.

Masood's words come to mind. He said, "For this spirit of human innovation, which will bring about the evolution of humanity on this planet, today you pay in dollars. In the past, people paid with sheepskin, spices, beans, wheat, etc. Tomorrow you will pay with whatever currency exists tomorrow."

The mistake most pundits make is that they are chronically confused. They cannot differentiate between the spirit of human innovation (at the heart of corporate America) and the United States dollar (American currency); they think it's one and the same. Many have hoarded gold or digital currency (Bitcoins, etc.), with a false belief that stocks (pieces of a company in which resides the spirit of human innovation) are nothing but US dollars/currency, and people run to safe havens like gold/Bitcoins to hedge against stock-market declines. These pundits have helped promote a common belief among people that the stock market is nothing but a casino.

Let me throw some light on this so our pundits can see.

> Dear pundits, it doesn't matter if you hoard cash, treasury bills, sheepskin, gold, or digital currency. It's only a modality of exchange to own real wealth, i.e., a piece of the spirit of human innovation. At any given time, the owner of this spirit will end up owning whatever the mode of transaction there is, whether it's dollars, Bitcoins, phantom coins, gold, sheepskin, wheat, poop coins, rice, coffee beans, etc. The gold standard of wealth is not gold—it's the spirit of human innovation, the ideas that are revolutionizing the world, for which people are willing to part with their money at any given time.

This wisdom that Ravi and Masood shared with me opened my eyes, and I never again looked at the stock market as a place of ticker symbols with a changing dollar value. I looked at it as a collection of pieces of companies; and at the heart of each of these companies were The Founders, The Doers, The Dreamers, and The Innovators, in whom resided the spirit of innovation. This perspective on the public companies (companies on the stock exchange) has made me wealthier. From that day onward, I have been a buyer of the best and brightest American companies, which are filled with the best and brightest minds that propel America forward.

### WHY DO THE RICH KEEP GETTING RICHER?

Imagine that there are two things you can choose from, but you can only choose one of them.

1. There is a golden crown with studded rubies and diamonds. It is the only one in the entire world, extremely valuable and rare. The only thing it can do is sit on your head and look amazing,
2. Ten percent ownership of a very successful interventional cardiologist. You will receive 10 percent of everything this cardiologist earns, you own 10 percent of whatever he invents, you own 10 percent of whichever new company he creates in the future, and you own 10 percent of whatever he buys in the future. The best part is this cardiologist is immortal.

Which of the two options would you choose?

Let's tweak it a little. What if there was a heart hospital that you owned, where 500 such immortal cardiologists existed. They were all immaculate. On a few occasions, a couple of them turned defective but were replaced with a couple of newer and better cardiologists, at no cost to you, practically for free. Some cardiologists outperformed everyone else. Some performed so-so. Some did very well, and a few did poorly, while all along you continued to reap the benefits of owning such a heart hospital.

Now what if you, your kids, your grandkids, and the generations to come continue to reap the benefits of the ownership of such a heart hospital, filled with the best 500 immortal cardiologists? What if there was no tax to pay to own this hospital, or any licensing fees? What if there was no need to borrow money to own such a wonderful heart hospital?

What would you choose?

Let's get out of the poor-man mentality now, and let's think as the wealthy do.

For a moment, imagine this heart hospital as your kingdom. You are the king, and the world's 500 best immortal cardiologists work for you.

Your ownership of their abilities, over time, will make you wealthier and wealthier.

With the productivity of these cardiologists, you will not only be rich but also far wealthier. Someday, using the returns from the productivity of these immortal cardiologists, you will own the crown (option 1) as well.

Essentially, by choosing option 2, a productive asset (a thing that pays you), you ended up owning a nonproductive asset (a thing that holds its value) as well, which is option 1 or the gold crown.

If only you had chosen option 1 earlier then.

Remember, all this time, your shiny crown sat on your head, looking amazing, and did nothing. During that same time, the immortal cardiologists were working relentlessly to make someone else wealthier.

By choosing a productive asset, you were not only wealthy but you also looked amazing, with a crown on your head.

Now in your mind, replace an immortal cardiologist with an American company.

And replace the gold crown with a nice luxury like a car or mansion.

This is the wisdom of the wealthy.

"Now, do you wonder why the rich keep getting richer and the poor keep getting poorer?" Ravi asked.

It's the choices people make, I thought. Some choose to own a piece of the spirit of human innovation (stock of an American company), while others choose to own shiny objects or fancy things (nonproductive things).

## THE PARANOID INVESTOR

Masood continued, "You will come across bat-shit, scared, emotional so-called investors. You will come across pundits who will claim they own crystal balls. You will also come across one more kind. I call them the "paranoids.""

The paranoids have one thing in common: they think everything is a conspiracy. They think everyone is coming after them; the world will come to an end, and we all need to prepare for the end of the world, not the biblical end or the judgment day that most scriptures talk about. It's their own convincing case for how the end of the world will look.

"A classic example is my colleague," Ravi said, "a nurse who is convinced that the stock market is rigged to rob the common man, and that it's a government conspiracy to purposefully keep the price of gold and silver low by selling derivatives on the market against these precious metals."

I recently texted Ravi to find out how his panicked friend was doing during the coronavirus pandemic.

Ravi told me that during these coronavirus panic days, his paranoid friend is convinced the world is ending and that the new world order has begun.

The paranoid investor decided to liquidate his entire retirement accounts (401(k) and IRAs) and took the money out, to buy gold and silver, as advised by a financial pundit.

This paranoid nurse was just another victim of a pundit and another case of being badly brainwashed with conspiracies.

He texted Ravi the other day, offering him protection if he needed help during these times of revolution.

Ravi said, "He told me he is at his cabin in northern Minnesota and is digging a trench around his cabin. He is also hoarding gold, silver, guns, and bullets. He said he will hunt and fish for food and grow food on his land and protect himself against anyone with the viral infection. If you listen to him carefully, he will convince you that the only way to save the economy is for the dollar to go back to gold standard. He'll talk in detail about how various civilizations in the past have ended. After listening to him, you may as well decide to buy a lake cabin in northern Minnesota, dig a trench around it, and hoard bullets, guns, gold, and silver, and maybe canned food."

Certainly, you will find many pundits in the media, scaring you so they can sell you some gold, silver, or imaginary digital coins (Bitcoins, aka electrons).

Brainwashed by other anti-stock pundits, people believe the whole market is rigged to steal money from the common man and put it into the pockets of the big banks.

I understand this concern very well, especially after what happened during the dot-com bubble and the 2008 housing crisis. While watching such market havoc and decline could be gut-wrenching, it is important to note that a great temperament can withstand paper losses (non-real loss if you did not get scared and sell your stock).

Remember, if the market was going down and you panicked and sold your stock, what would have been a paper loss would turn into a realized loss (real loss). When a market is going down, remember to sit back, preferably turn the news off, never sell, and if you have some money saved, consider buying some more stock.

Never buy on margin or borrowed money. Because if you do, then when the market crashes, the person who lent you money will expect you to sell what you bought and will ask you to pay up. This is one of the most important reasons people lose money in a stock market crash.

## WHEN IS THE MARKET OVERVALUED?

Masood shared some more wisdom. "Remember the words of Carl Sagan. 'If we do not destroy ourselves, we will venture to the stars.'"

Then he continued to say, "If humanity did go to the extreme of destroying itself, what would be the worth of owning all the gold and Bitcoin, or all the paintings on this planet, or the planet itself? If humanity did venture to the stars, what is your gold worth on earth anyway? Don't you want to own a piece of that human spirit of innovation, which will take us to the stars?"

Masood said, "I will tell you, however, what will be more valuable than all the gold and Bitcoin combined. It's a piece of the spirit of human innovation, which will take us to the stars someday."

Do you want to know what it's worth?

More than all the shiny metal and electrons (digital currency, coins, Bitcoins, etc.) on this entire planet.

Ravi said, "Those shiny bars of precious metal were mined, minted, and purified by machines and chemicals created by the human mind. The necklace around your neck, or the designer, precious-metal bangles/bracelets around your wrists are also the result of the spirit of human innovation; so is the creation of Bitcoin, and other digital currencies, through technology that was created by the spirit of human innovation."

Clearly there is a huge difference between a human's ability to create and his creation. What you want to own is the mind's ability to create, not its creation.

Indeed, the spirit of human innovation, captured in all companies, is priceless. There is no proper yardstick to measure the value or worth of a company without knowing the impact of changes it will create with its innovative minds. I would conclude this argument by saying this: the stock market is not undervalued or overvalued. It is just valued. You may also say it is the touchstone that will help you determine the value of every other asset out there. The spirit of innovation, captured in companies, is the absolute scale of value against which every other asset should be measured. It's the only thing constant and the only thing of true value in a free market, with the exception of "time."

## THE ROLE OF GOLD

Masood said, "Note that I am not against buying some physical precious metal. I am against the reason why people are hoarding it. They are hoarding it for all the wrong reasons. There is one reason I would recommend buying some physical precious metal, physical gold only and not paper gold."

Physical gold and paper gold? I only knew the physical, gold jewelry that my mother wore in India, the gold bangles, necklaces, and other gold jewelry and physical gold that she inherited from my grandmother. I always thought paper gold was the equivalent of physical gold, until Masood broadened my horizons.

Remember this, said Masood, "If there comes a time when humanity destroys itself and does not succeed 100 percent, no technology will exist. Your grandchildren and generations to come should have something to trade with, to rebuild their wealth. Physical gold and silver serve the purpose of tax-free inheritance, passed on from generations to future generations, as in Indian culture. In many other cultures, children aren't allowed to sell their inherited gold, but should continue to hold it and pass it on to their children and so on. Physical gold serves as the best insurance against a catastrophe if it does happen, not your GLD or your IAU, your Bitcoin, or other digital currency (i.e., poop). One should hold enough physical precious metal, which you can hold and touch, not to trade but as a hedge against man-made catastrophes, as an insurance one can use to rebuild his or her wealth."

## DIGITAL CURRENCY VERSUS GOLD

I always wondered why Masood said digital currency was equivalent to poop. It makes total sense now. God forbid that a disaster (man-made, or natural like a solar storm), as described by Masood, did happen and humanity did not succeed in destroying itself 100 percent. In the absence of technology, your ownership of digital currency is only worth electrons, and what is the worth of an electron in the absence of technology anyway?

"Masood, you just convinced me to hold some physical gold in my investment portfolio," Ravi said.

*What wisdom*, I thought. These men were not just successful, smart investors but smart hedgers too. They were humble enough to listen and question each other's wisdom; their cups were always empty. They were always thirsty for more knowledge. They had their feet in reality while dreaming of an innovative world, for the betterment of all humanity. They never counted their dollars but were far wealthier than most. I was in the company of unique men, better men than myself.

Masood said, "The pundit who sells you the idea of trading gold for creation of wealth is just in love with your hard-earned, post-tax US dollars; that's all."

"What about those money managers or wealth advisors who advise you to add some paper gold to your portfolio?" I asked.

"Those pundits who recommend adding paper gold to your portfolio, like gold ETFs (useless market instruments that produce nothing), want to sell this to you because they have a profound attraction to your hard-earned, post-tax dollars," Masood said. "Or they simply don't know the purpose of physical gold."

## BITCOINS AND SPECULATION

Why are people hoarding Bitcoin?

Precisely because they do not understand stocks.

Imagine you own a ten-acre farmland. Every year you grow wheat, cotton, corn, or soybeans. That land is productive land because it's producing something.

Or suppose you owned Coca-Cola stock or Apple stock; the company you own is producing a drink or a phone, respectively.

What does Bitcoin or digital currency produce?

How is Bitcoin, or any other digital currency, different from, say, an expensive painting on this planet, created by a human mind? You may love a painting and buy it for $150 million (good for you!). What does that painting provide for me? Which one of my problems does it solve? Bitcoin is just like the painting, which produces nothing and solves no problem, or a piece of gold that does nothing but sit there and look shiny. A Bitcoin does nothing and produces nothing.

Just because something went up in value does not mean it's necessarily a good investment.

If people are buying because it's going up, they probably want to sell it to someone after it has gone up. If the person to whom you sold it is thinking the same, or they bought it because someone will buy it from them for a higher price, that's a sign of trouble.

The wisdom of the wealthy cautions you against such investments.

## DECREASE YOUR LIABILITIES (THINGS THAT COST YOU MONEY)

The first thing you must remember is this: it doesn't matter how much you earn; what matters is how much you keep by saving or decreasing your liabilities and/or by increasing your income. Increase your income, decrease your liabilities, and invest the difference in assets (things that pay you). That is the key to building long-term wealth.

Think of that latest phone or the second car you don't use much; that boat or RV that just sits there looking pretty; that motorcycle you didn't need; and many more things that you thought you needed but truly don't. You still have a payment on them, you still incur the cost of registration, insurance, maintenance, etc.

Anything that you don't need but which costs you money is a liability. The lower your liability, the more money you save every month.

There are some expenses you just cannot escape. Some pundits claim your house is a liability. While it may be, I don't expect you to sell your home and live under a rock.

If you did not buy a house, you would still be paying rent for a roof over your head. It's just one of life's necessities.

There are certain things you need to live a decent life. I just call them life's necessities, not liabilities.

Taxes are one of your biggest liabilities.

Some financial pundits (self-proclaimed experts) encourage you not to pay your taxes and to take shortcuts. Don't listen to such pundits. These experts claim they paid zero in taxes. Don't aspire to be like them. Don't learn their shenanigans, but seek counsel from good tax advisors. If your deductions are so high that you end up paying zero in taxes, so be it. But if you are blessed by the Creator to have made a good amount of money via income (earned or through investments) and/or capital gain (money made after selling an asset for profit), don't be stingy. Pay your due share toward the betterment of this society. I am not suggesting that you over- or underpay your taxes, but pay your due share. Be a good citizen of the country that protects your rights and mine. Your country ensures this peace and harmony because there are free markets for you and me to participate in. Your honesty also helps protect that single mother who is working two jobs to make ends meet.

Your second biggest liability is money borrowed for the purchase of liabilities—your credit card debt, your car loan, lease payments, and other forms of debt that went into buying things that don't pay you an income.

These are worse liabilities because, not only are you paying interest on those loans, but those things you bought are slowly losing value over time. Whether you use or do not use them, they still cost you money to maintain.

A good example is your second car, whether you leased it or bought it. You will possibly have a lease payment or a loan payment on it. A car is a liability because once you have used it, it cannot be sold for the price for which you purchased it. It simply went down in value the moment you drove it out of the showroom. Whether you use it or don't, you pay insurance, registration, maintenance, fuel, etc.

All this while your car has made you no money but keeps consuming the money you have made by other means, like your job.

If you earned $1,000 (your asset), and you incur $1,000 in expenses (your liabilities), you have kept zero dollars. Hence, your net worth is zero.

If your assets are greater than your liabilities, your net worth is positive.

If your liabilities are greater than your assets, your net worth is negative.

The wealthy have only one scorecard, and it's called net worth. The higher your net worth, the wealthier you are.

Net worth is a true measure of wealth, and it's calculated by subtracting all you owe from everything you own.

An important step to wealth is keeping the wealth scorecard called net worth.

## COLLECT ASSETS

What are assets? Simply defined, they are things that increase your net worth and make you wealthier over time.

Assets are things that pay you, for example rental real estate that pays you rent; a business you own that is profitable enough to pay you, the owner, money (cash flow); dividend-paying stocks, or stocks that don't pay dividends but have good earnings; and interest paying bonds, etc.

Your job or your work that pays you an income is also an asset.

If your financial adviser says bad things about being employed and suggests that you quit your job, steer clear from such financial PUNDITS.

Do not quit your job. There is a correct way to transition from being employed into becoming an entrepreneur in pursuit of your American dream. We will talk about it in another section.

## MONEY BEGETS MONEY

How do you collect assets?

For example, imagine you earned a salary of $1,000, and you spent $500 on life's necessities and taxes. Then you are left with $500 in savings.

With this $500, if you bought shiny objects, clothes, fancy suits, new phones, shoes, paintings, etc., you essentially have collected liabilities, which cost you money. They will sit there and not pay you anything.

But what if you used that $500 to go out there and earn more money for yourself?

Think of your saved $500 as 500 hard-working people working to hire more hard-working people to work for you. These people work for you. They don't eat or sleep. They work all day and all night.

This is the wisdom of the wealthy, and this is how the wealthy think.

If you develop this wealth-building mindset, you will be wealthy too.

The wealthy, just like you, also saved $500, but instead of buying shiny objects, etc., they would research and find an asset they could buy that pays them.

For example, there are many dividend-paying ETF's priced between $25–$100 that pay a dividend yield anywhere between 4–6 percent annually.

You, with a wealthy mindset, will buy such an asset.

What then?

Your $500 may have appreciated (gone up in value) by about 10 percent. The same stock of ETF is now worth $550, while during the same year, for buying such an asset, you were paid 5 percent in dividends. You were paid $25 (dividends) for buying something (an asset). That same asset is now worth $550.

Your net worth is now $550, plus you are now getting paid $25.

It doesn't matter how you spend the $25 you received as a dividend, because this asset pays you again and again and again, like a golden goose laying a golden egg.

Now use that $25 to buy the shiny shoes or tie or whatever you like, because an asset pays you over and over and over again.

Now you will never run out of money.

Imagine if you did this every month, collecting more assets, earning more dollars to recruit more dollars, which go out there to recruit more dollars. Now the earned dollars and the recruited dollars go out there and recruit more dollars for you; all this while your dollars did this work for you, while you worked and focused on increasing your income. While you chilled, your dollars worked hard. While you played, your dollars worked harder. While you worked, your dollars worked harder. Finally, when you don't want to work, your dollars continue to work for you, forever and ever and ever.

How can anyone stop you from being wealthy when you have an army of dollars working for you, day in and day out, even while you sleep?

Have you heard of the phrase, "The rich make money while they sleep?" Have you ever wondered how?

## INVESTMENT METHODS

There are several methods for investing in the stock market.

Let's take a look at patterns and technical analysis.

Most commonly, you will hear pundits talking about patterns. These pundits will go to great lengths talking about these patterns and trends. They will share stories about their success buying XYZ stock or ABC stock and how it broke out (a specific pattern before the stock goes up very fast), and they made a fortune in five minutes. Steer clear and away from these kinds of experts. If you find the one who talks about patterns, push your fingers deep into your external ear canals and disappear. You will not create everlasting wealth and enjoy the blessings of life by following this investment method.

At the same time, using this technique, with a stroke of luck and a 50/50 chance, you will find a breakout stock and make some money. Then with the same 50/50 probability, you'll lose some money. You might win more than you lose, so you might make some money, or lose more than you win, and possibly lose what you have.

Most importantly, you will spend one hell of a time researching these patterns, which is quality time away from family or a nice hike during which you could enjoy a sunrise or sunset. There is more to life than trading stocks; that is "life" itself. There is one and only one true commodity in life: time. Once spent, it never comes back. Time always runs in one direction. Think about it.

Indeed, very precious and in limited quantity is one's time. If you choose to spend it looking at a screen or some pattern, all day, years from now you will realize the author of this book was right, and you should have just listened to the wisdom of Ravi, Masood, and Mervin.

## INVESTING BASED ON FUNDAMENTALS AND VALUE-BASED INVESTING

In this method, you analyze a company's financial statements and make assumptions of its future prospects, earnings potentials, etc.

This method is used, to some extent, by some of the most successful investors in the world, like Warren Buffett, who would buy companies with a durable competitive advantage (something special about one company that cannot be easily replicated by others) and hold them, long-term, to create massive wealth.

This method could be subdivided into an approach called the short(sell)-long(buy) approach. For example, you analyze a company and find its financials very appealing. You project that its earnings will grow with excellent future prospects. You also believe the company demonstrates an excellent, durable competitive advantage. You decide to go long (buy) on its stock.

(Durable competitive advantage: a competitive edge of a company or a sustainable factor that provides a business an edge over its competitors.)

Then you analyze another company and find the company is losing money, has a horrible management team, is losing market share, and has no competitive advantage. You believe this company will continue to lose money in the foreseeable future. So you decide to short (to sell stock without buying it before) its stock.

Wisdom from this author: based on these assumptions, you will either make or lose money; the probabilities may slightly favor your assumptions. However, it's important to remember that a dirty company could pivot and correct itself and become profitable. Or a very good company, due to an unseen, low-probability event, could lose money, for example, airline companies in the COVID-19 pandemic or what happened to Boeing after the 747 Max crash.

Ravi continued. "Among them are some that invest based on the ability to see an event that the general market is unable to see. These individuals take a short position on the market and wait for the psychological market parameters to occur. Once the event is clearly witnessed by all market participants and the fear subsides, these individuals cover (close) their short positions and happily walk to the bank. To the untrained eye, these individuals appear godly and somehow able to predict the peak of the market, or to know when the market is over-valued and due for a correction. But to a trained eye, these individuals are just those well-researched souls who predict market reactions based on the impact of a specific event or multiple events."

That's right; some names came to my mind who had predicted the 2008 crisis accurately.

At the end of the day, you have to remember: no matter how excellent your ability to read a balance sheet may be, investment in the market is a game of psychological strength. It's the most brutal test ever invented to test human temperament in modern history—without, of course, direct jeopardy to human life. The market can instill fear to a degree never seen or experienced by a human (i.e., the market can create fear equivalent to being eaten by a lion, without being eaten by a lion). If you are fainthearted and cannot withstand massive market declines and cannot sleep peacefully after seeing your portfolio cut by 50 percent, maybe the stock market is not for you. Better to buy a less volatile invest-ment and spare yourself a myocardial infarction.

Less volatile investment: an investment whose market value does not change much on a day-to-day basis.

## MR. MARKET: THE PSYCHOLOGICAL COMPONENT OF ANY MARKET

Masood added, "However, it's important to draw your atten-tion to the wisdom of Charlie Munger, Warren Buffet, and his teacher, Benjamin Graham, who came up with a name for this market psychological menace. They called it 'Mr. Market' in Mr. Graham's famous books. I just merely call it the psychological component of any market."

To every market, such as a meat market, wheat market, housing market, or stock market, there are two components.

1. The fundamental component
2. The psychological component

This is why two types of people make money in any market.

Which two types?

The first type understands the fundamental aspects (numbers, earning prospects, future potential, etc.). They are able to point out irrational behavior and buy the investments that become available for a lower price. Or in other words, they buy businesses at a buying price lower than the intrinsic (true market) value of the business.

The second type of investors who make money in any market are the ones who understand human psychology, behavior, and how humans behave together (mass psychology). These individuals may or may not have a (psychology, psychiatry, medical) health-care background, or these could be individuals who have observed markets over a long period of time. These individuals then point out bubbles (irrational optimism) in the market and then look for events that could deflate this market bubble. Once they are able to point out this event, they generally tend to short (bet against) the market, then wait for all market participants (stock buyers and sellers) to panic and deflate the bubble. Once the market is deflated, they are able to gauge market fear and then close the short positions (close all bets) and go long (this also means to then buy up the stock market, at the bottom, before it starts going up).

## TEMPERAMENT IS KEY TO RICHES

Essentially it takes a great deal of discipline to bet for or against millions of humans participating in a market, and their behaviors.

For example, if you owned a beautiful home, imagine you bought it for $1 million, and a realtor comes to you and says, "So-and-so wants to buy your house for $250,000."

Would you then get scared that your house had dropped in value and sell your house? Or would you say, "I don't care, and I am not interested in selling my house"?

But what if the same realtor came back, the next day, and said that a bunch of buyers really love your home, and one of them would like to pay you $5 million in cash right now? Would you consider maybe selling your house? Possibly, yes!

If you would make such logical decisions with the ownership of your home, then why is there a different logic when it comes to ownership of the world's best companies through the stock market?

Is it because the agent on the stock market is giving you a stock quote each second?

Remember, sometimes the stock quote is too high, and sometimes it's too low.

It doesn't mean you have to buy or sell because a certain change in price has occurred.

Why does the market price of a stock change so much?

Remember that there are all kinds of people trading stocks. Some are bipolar (manic and depressed). Some are just chronically depressed, and some forever manic.

They attach all kinds of their own psychological emotions into the price of a stock, selling and buying with their mood swings.

When they get scared or depressed and sell too much (the stock market goes down), you bet against their gloomy emotion and buy their stock. When they become manic and buy too much (stock market goes up), be cautious and maybe bet against their mania by selling your stock to them.

## MARKET BUBBLE

Sometimes the free markets are taken over by overly optimistic (manic behavior) market participants (stock buyers). These market participants (stock traders, buyers, and sellers) buy stocks/commodities, etc., with the sole intention of selling them to someone else at a higher price. This phenomenon continues for some time, and a specific company or commodity continues to create new highs (it goes up and up in value) until this bubble bursts. Usually when the buyers are unable to sell at a higher price, they then start selling at whatever price they can. This results in the lofty stock/ETF/commodity valuation (price) crashing downward. This is also called bursting the bubble.

This bubble-like feature is especially worrisome as more people are buying Bitcoin/digital currency today for the same reason.

Ask anyone buying a Bitcoin or digital currency the reason for their purchase. They will say, "Because it's going up in value."

Now ask them, what does Bitcoin produce?

Nothing. That's right. It produces nothing.

I would rather buy a farm that produces some corn than buy a nonproductive asset (Bitcoin or digital currency), which produces nothing.

## MARRY THE FUNDAMENTALS TO HUMAN PSYCHOLOGY

To properly understand the market, understanding psychology seems absolutely critical.

Being good with numbers and psychology is one hell of a combination. Once a journalist asked Charlie Munger if he was concerned that Berkshire Hathaway stock was down 50 percent. Charlie Munger replied that his concern was zero. That, my friend, is a lethal combination of fundamentals and rock-solid temperament, strengthened by a profound understanding of human psychology.

If you have already been investing in the stock market, you would have realized that by now.

Even after extensive research, companies with exceptional financials may not have produced the desired returns. Even with a long-term perspective in mind, you may have failed to realize the desired result. You may have come across multiple articles in which a person throwing darts on a list of stocks, while blindfolded, has done better than active stock-picking experts.

If you are a trader, you might have scratched your head and wondered, What is the right approach to beat the stock market consistently, all this while wondering what would have happened if you had just stuck to a simple dollar-cost averaging into an index strategy. Then maybe you would not have lost the amount of money you already had.

If you have read this book, so far, you will be honest and know, in your own heart and mind, that neither you nor I, the author of this book, is as smart as Dr. Michael Burry MD, who spotted the peak of the market, during the subprime mortgage crisis of 2008–2009 and in the current Coronavirus pandemic crisis of 2020, with pinpoint accuracy. You will also acknowledge the fact that you and I don't tap dance to our investment world like Mr. Warren Buffett.

Now you could be as brilliant as Warren Buffet and buy the bottom, as the market goes to the dogs, or you may be as smart as Dr. Michael Burry and find the top, short it, exploit the psychological component of the market participants, and wait for the magic to unravel. There is no right or wrong approach; they have both made money. You may choose to short the top and buy the bottom or buy the bottom and hold to the top. Both will make money provided you can replicate the approach.

But can you?

Furthermore, can you withstand the gut wrench if your positions moved against you?

I personally, who like to wake up late, would rather tap dance to work in the afternoon. I would rather take a buy-and-hold approach than take a short position and lose sleep.

There is one approach, however, which you could use consistently to come out profitable every time, more or less, potentially even beating the market, without being an expert at any of it.

"Do you then not need to be an expert at financials or psychology?" I asked.

Ravi shook his head. "You need to be familiar with both. There is no replacement to acquiring knowledge and learning. Of the two components of the market, I recommend becoming extremely strong at the psychological component. The psychological component is generally the harder of the two to master. With the fundamental aspect, as long as you don't make massive errors on good, publicly traded companies, you may still be okay. If you are weak at analyzing individual companies, you could potentially employ this strategy onto index ETFs, for example SPY, etc. In this manner, you would not have to worry about individual stocks, their earnings, or the bad or good news affecting the pricing of their underlying stock. A stock moving in the opposite direction of your assumption or position will cause you pain, especially if your assumption turns out to be the wrong one."

Warren Buffet once said that, only when the tide goes out, do you discover who has been swimming naked. I would say, "Don't be that naked person."

Do a little research, and look around you. There are examples of booms and busts everywhere. There are thousands of funds that have gone bust using excess leverage (borrowed money), unable to withstand drawdowns (sudden market crashes); these were the ones caught naked when the tide went away. If you gave your money to these naked swimming champions, you would have been forced to sell your clothes too. Then imagine joining them in a naked swimming competition with a goal to drown the fastest. Giving your money to someone else to manage it is like having your sheep looked after by a wolf. What do you expect, the sheep to grow in number? You can look up countless examples of how fund managers charge exorbitant fees and perform poorly, repeatedly, even in bull (up-trending) markets. You would have been better off just sticking your money into an index fund, riding this market roller coaster, and still coming out ahead in the long run.

Exceptionally researched hindsight and application of such knowledge, acquired by careful observation, is always mistaken for amazing foresight. One's prediction must be substantiated with a combination of experience, assessment of probabilities, and exceptionally researched hindsight. If it's not, don't waste your time listening to this so-called expert advice.

The examples are as follows:

"Over many years, our ancestors learned to avoid the route where a lion always hunted its prey. They learned the behavior of predators and avoided the bushes under which those predators commonly hid or rested. Some of our ancestors never cared to do their due diligence; hence, they never bothered to look under those bushes/trees to make sure there were no sleeping lions/tigers, etc. They decided to walk through the forest anyway," Ravi said. "Now guess what happened to those ancestors who never did their due diligence?"

"They had a very short life span," I said softly.

"They were eaten," Masood said. "And they were probably not our ancestors. They were stupid and never lived long enough to have enough offspring."

Who is the best decision maker for yourself?

If there was a life-or-death decision to be made and the person making that decision for you was you, then naturally you would choose what was best for you. Unless you were suicidal and restrained in a psychiatric ward, you would obviously choose life. What if your important life decision was made by someone who didn't care much about your well-being?

That sounds painful.

Would you be comfortable having that person continue to make such decisions for you? What if someone else raised your kids and didn't care much about their well-being? Would you be OK with that idea and continue to live with it?

If you would not let your kids be raised by someone else, why would you trust someone else with your future, your life, and your life savings?

Giving your money away, for someone else to manage, is similar to having someone else make life-and-death decisions for you. I guess people who love their lives and their families learn to manage money themselves.

"I was freshly graduated from residency, and after a couple of months, a money manager came to me offering services for a 2 percent management fee," Masood said. "He said he knew a lot more about money than I did and could do an excellent job. I made the mistake of giving my money to him. A few years later, the amount of money I gave him lost 10 percent in value while, during the same period, the S&P 500 Index had gone upwards close to 35 percent. I thought to myself, something was wrong. So I decided to speak to my money manager. He gave me multiple reasons as to why he did poorly, and he, most importantly, demonstrated why: I was incapable of managing my own money, and managing money was the hardest job on the planet.

He explained to me that I was a busy physician, that my time was better served taking care of patients and that managing money was not for me. Furthermore, this manager had a finance degree from a reputed business school. I asked why his performance was below standard. He replied, 'Managing money is the toughest job on the planet.' To this manager, I said, 'If you think managing money is hard, you should try saving a life.' That day I fired the manager, took my money, learned to manage my own money, and in sixteen months, I became a millionaire."

If you can work hard enough to feed your family, you can learn to manage your own money. It's not rocket science.

"Why would you listen to pundits and money managers, without doing your own due diligence, and let them drive your future and prosperity?" asked Masood, still feeling the past pain and agony. The source of his discomfort was clearly the money manager. "If you do not know how to raise a kid, you learn. If you do not know how to handle and invest money, you make the effort to learn. Do the due diligence, and look under the bush, and check the path you are taking. Make sure there are no lions, and make sure that the path is taking you to your destiny. Expecting someone else to do it for you is just like—"

"Just like having your sheep be watched over by a wolf. Your sheep are surely getting fleeced and worse, eaten," said Mervin, finishing his sentence.

Some of these fund managers tie their compensations to a percentage of profits; this makes them take higher leverage (borrow more money) and take higher risks, to demonstrate better results. This is just greed, nothing else.

If they created a higher return, is that not good?

Well, it is if they can do it consistently.

The problem is, because of this excess leverage (borrowed money), they are unable to survive massive drawdowns (sudden market collapse), and soon, they go belly up. There are two great enemies of humankind: greed and fear. It's greed that enables these fund managers and individual investors to take on higher risk and leverage, whatever may be the reason—underlying hunger for more money or for fame. Looking at such outstanding performances, some investors throw more money at such fund/firm managers and then, when the ship (the manager) goes down, so does the fund and all the investors who invested in it.

Then there is another form of greed. This greed is the catalyst to fear of missing out (FOMO), especially when markets rally (quick movement upwards) upwards every day. It becomes more and more difficult to sit on the sidelines waiting for the market to return to fair value. Even the most seasoned investors make this mistake. Time and time again these greed-catalyst investors catch the peak of the market (top) and ride the painful journey downward (riding a market crash downward); this is followed by a slow recovery if they are blessed with temperament and are strong on the psychological aspects.

However, if they are not strong on temperament or psychology, they are the first to quit. When witnessing paper losses (non-real loss), some sell and run, at the wrong time, realizing real losses (jumping off stock market roller coasters). Then there are the other greed catalysts who catch this peak. They suddenly become fearful, when the market moves in the other direction, and their greed turns to massive fear. They sell everything and then incur massive losses that you read about in newspapers.

"I have seen this over and over again," Masood said. "Then what happens is that there are more and more who catch this contagious fear of a dropping market, until it turns into a widespread panic and sell is the word on every lip. Take your money and run is also the word on every lip. It's precisely when you witness a freely falling market that tremendous opportunities are created for the ones who are patient and for the ones who never swim naked. These cycles of boom-and-bust happen in every market. The more participation in any market, the more pronounced the cycle. This is an aspect of human psychology and will never change, as long as humans continue to trade financial stock, housing, or in any market."

(Never swim naked means never invest in stocks with borrowed money.)

It seemed to me as though Ravi and Masood could walk into

the minds of human traders, gather thoughts from their minds, and make unbiased decisions. How do they achieve that level of psychological temperament? I wondered.

Ravi then said, "Never buy or sell on margin (borrowed money), because you never know what will happen. This is a random world, and anything can happen."

His words ring in my mind today. No one expected a COVID-19 pandemic or an oil-price war, and no one will predict the next random event. Ravi's words were always true.

You can be absolutely sure that the next random event will affect everyone and everything you know or care about. Remember this every time your inner self tries to drive you crazy with greed, especially when your buddies have success stories of how they doubled their money on one ABC stock.

Remind yourself of Murphy's Law. "Nothing is as easy as it looks, everything takes longer than you expect, if anything can go wrong, it will go wrong...and at the worst possible moment."

If possible, remind your buddies too. Always put money aside for emergencies. Keep money to run your household expenses and obligations for at least two to three months. Always buy and keep term life insurance. Do not over-leverage (do not borrow more than you need), and always keep your debts on rental real estate and other assets manageable. When investing in the stock market, psychologically train your mind to know that if you do not see your money or stock price for the next ten to fifteen years, you will still be comfortable; no news from the financial markets will disturb your sleep at night. Psychologically train your mind to know that if your stock holding went to zero, this would not affect an ounce of your inner peace. If your investment affects the way you make decisions and live your life, you need to fix your life and bring your family and personal life in order before you seek millions from investing. Once this level of mental/psychological temperament is attained, you are ready for the markets. Without this psychological temperament, you are only as good and as ready as a running, headless chicken is for dinner.

Is there any other way to invest in a market, independent of your own and other human psychological bias?

Yes, there is. One of the first methods is dollar-cost averaging a fixed amount of money into the market, at regular intervals, and ignoring the market moves. As you dollar-cost average a fixed amount, the amount buys more shares, as the market goes down, and buys fewer shares as the market goes up. Overall this gives you a satisfactory return, over a long period of time, in the market. It is not the act of timing the market but the time spent in the market that matters. No one can safely and accurately predict what will happen in the markets tomorrow or, say, in a week or a month, but it can be reasonably assumed that overall, over a long period of time, the spirit of human innovation will only become more and more valuable, relative to any other nonproductive asset. It is important to note that, over an extended period of time, mutual funds will underperform index fund ETFs, likely because of the cost and fees associated with mutual funds. Also important to note is that a mutual fund is managed and run by a human money manager, and his temperament will also be tested to the fullest, without a doubt. A manager is not free from of greed, catalytic greed, the urge to outperform other fund managers, or fear of underperformance. His/her urge to cut losses and run like everyone else will cost you over an extended period. A fund manager is only human and will underperform an electronically traded fund, over an extended period of time, without a doubt.

Now you can make a choice; either you find a money manager who demonstrates an ideal temperament, like Charlie Munger or Warren Buffet, or train yourself psychologically to attain this ideal temperament. It is a lot easier to train yourself than to find and bet on a future Warren or Charlie.

Many fund managers take pride in their ability to stock pick.

Trust me, most of these managers demonstrate exceptional knowledge of the financial markets. Their skill at analyzing and interpreting financial statements and theories of future earnings growth, and their convincing assumptions of durable competitive advantage, will dwarf all the knowledge you and I will ever accumulate, and they will still underperform the market. This has been demonstrated by these managers' inability to consistently outperform the market. Somehow these guys manage to keep losing your money and still keep their jobs. It's probably because they have convinced you that they know more about the market than you do, and you have decided to believe them. The fact is, anyone who claims to accurately predict the market moves is not only deceiving himself/herself but also deceiving you, either knowingly or unknowingly. They will take you down the drain with them and will fleece, or worse, eat your sheep when they are hungry.

*It ain't what you don't know that gets you into trouble. It's what you know for sure that just ain't so. (Mark Twain)*

## THE SOPHISTICATED INVESTOR
### APPROACH INDEPENDENT OF BIASES

Once, a wise person said, "Always take care of your downside. The upside will take care of itself." I took this to heart. As I invested, I always ensured that my cost of getting into a stock/ETF position was lower, and once a position was established, I ensured that I never lost money.

This is achieved by hedging (protecting) positions and then by continuing to decrease the cost of getting into such a (stock or ETF) position.

This I learned from Ravi, and it was not easy. It took time and temperament before I could drive my investments on cruise control. The only reason I lost some money is that I did not listen to Ravi's advice. At times I became greedy and took on more leverage; I became fearful when the market tested my temperament.

Ravi said, "I am not as concerned about making a positive return. But I am very concerned about losing money. Remember, if you never lose money, eventually you will make some. This idea has helped me immensely, and I am sharing some of these ideas to help make a difference in your investing life as well."

When I heard Ravi say this, I was sitting there looking at the campfire. I was wondering if this was another lesson on a conservative investing strategy with probably paltry returns. I was wrong.

What I am trying to explain is a strategy that has consistently beaten markets and has performed outstandingly; it has provided a positive return, sometimes in double digits, on the entire portfolio, even during severe market declines with the ugliest downturns or crashes. Most importantly, this strategy works without using leverage/margin (borrowed money) or swimming naked (the act of trading in the market on margin).

(Using margin is the act of borrowing money from your brokerage to trade in the market.)

This section is recommended for the following types of individuals:

1. Professional/sophisticated investors
2. Investors determined to do better at investing in the stock market
3. Investors wanting to beat/outperform the market
4. Not recommended for the novice investor (beginner)

Note: my hope with the information I am conveying through this book is to help improve your general knowledge. It's not investment advice in itself; I am not an investment advisor. Furthermore, this is not the only successful approach to investing. The reader is not obligated to read or follow the advice. This section is for education only. Furthermore, using this approach, one may make or lose money. The author takes no responsibility for your losses and seeks no percentage of your profits. Profitability relies on individual wisdom of the markets, knowledge, and understanding. It is the responsibility of the reader of this book to acquire more education on topics discussed in this book for better understanding of the information presented.

Sophisticated/Advanced investors, please refer to Appendix section 3.

## FOLLOW THE BRAINS

After all the talk on the spirit of human innovation, and after understanding that one should never bet against the American spirit of innovation, there was a question in my mind that persistently annoyed me.

I decided to ask, "How can one assume everything will remain perfect forever? How can one assume the market will continue to increase in value forever? What if it does not? Where is the end?"

Mervin picked up on my question and said, "What you mean to ask is, will the spirit of human innovation continue to remain valuable, and will it continue to become more valuable in the future?"

Ravi said, "I believe the question is: when do you bet against America or its spirit of innovation?"

"When to bet against America!" Masood took a deep breath. "I would never bet against America or its ability to innovate. So far if you had bet against the United States, you may have lost your shirt, pants, and all your clothes and would have been running around naked."

Ravi said, "Masood is right. One should never bet against America. However there will come a time when you should bet against the United States, and that will make you very wealthy; now is certainly not the time, but watch for these signs."

The only reason the US is extremely successful is that it has always attracted the best and brightest from all over the world, for centuries. That means the United States has taken direct advantage of the innovative abilities of the world's best and brightest, to enrich itself. These brains have come to the United States and worked hard and helped build trillion-dollar companies. This has been a relationship that has been advantageous to both the inventor/entrepreneur/asset/immigrant and the United States itself.

Masood said, "It is true that, for centuries, the best and the brightest have left their home countries and have come to the United States in pursuit of the American dream."

The best scientists, athletes, doctors, engineers, inventors, entrepreneurs, managers, etc., came to the United States in pursuit of their American dream. They have enriched the economy with innovation and entrepreneurship. Watch out for a discontinuation in this pattern.

When this trend changes and the United States starts losing its best and brightest to other countries, it will be time to bet against America and go long, or buy that other country's innovative ability that captures this talent, which will flee America.

Long: to buy

Short: to sell

"This doesn't make sense. Why would talent leave America?" I asked.

Mervin replied, "If the promised American dream is not fulfilled, and when other countries demonstrate better immigration policies and start attracting talent."

Ravi said, "If you look carefully, Australia, Canada, and New Zealand have already adopted a fairer immigration system. Many scientists, doctors, and engineers in the United States are stuck in an unfair immigration system with decade-long backlogs. They are in wait lines for their green cards, and their lines run for decades because of age-old immigration rules that discriminate against people based on country of birth. These long immigration waiting lines will naturally push talent to countries that have fairer immigration systems. The day you start seeing massive brain drain out of the United States is the time to go "long" to the country that captures this talent.

Maybe just maybe, do not be "long" or even go "short" on the United States' innovative ability (corporate America). If the United States loses its talent and the innovative, ambitious brains move out of the country, the American economy may never recover. If you are following the news, the UK has also begun to adopt a fairer immigration system. If the United States does not promptly evolve, adapt, and start valuing its talent, in a few years the American success story as it exists today will slowly crumble and perish.

If the United States successfully adopts a "real," fair/merit-based system, free of discrimination based on country of birth, and keeps its best and brightest and continues to attract the best and brightest, then for many generations to come, there will be no economy that will match the might of the United States. But if the United States fails to evolve, it will stand no chance against the innovation that will happen in the countries that have adopted a better immigration system to attract the world's best and brightest. The United States will not be able to keep up or compete with innovation in other countries.

The United States immigration policy has, for many years, made it difficult for the best and brightest to immigrate into the United States. Sometimes its leaders go to the extent of blocking talented immigrants. They have also pushed away the best and brightest talent from our own best universities, back to their home countries, simply to appeal to their political agenda. This (the cutting of legal immigration) has hurt and will continue to hurt innovation in the United States. This is precisely the reason other countries have begun to innovate using the talent that they have captured. This very talent, now innovating in other countries, was pushed out of the USA, simply because of our poor immigration policies. To make America truly great, we need to welcome smart and bright immigrants. We cannot make or continue to keep America great by pushing our own brains and talent out of our own country into other countries.

Mervin said, "Today, the immigration system in the United States has become an agenda for partisan politics. While a nephrologist from India (a legal immigrant), who is the only nephrologist for three counties in Indiana, has a wait time of thirty years for a green card, the political discussions revolve around other hot, illegal-immigration-related, vote-swaying agendas."

If you believe the USA will continue to remain the innovative capital of the world, while the best and the brightest cannot own intellectual or commercial property or start businesses, think again. If the US immigration system continues to break down further and continues to show a cold shoulder to the best and the brightest, you may want to start diversifying your portfolio a little bit, with companies in countries that have a better immigration system in place. Without a doubt the smartest engineer will start the next Amazon or Facebook there, and without a doubt, the best doctors will be providing healthcare there, and the best and newest medications or vaccines will be invented there instead of in the USA.

Masood said, "Simply, I must say, watch for the brain drain, and follow the brains."

# Chapter 4

# INVESTING IN REAL ESTATE

Mervin, at age thirty-five, is an avid real estate investor; he owns several properties and has a net worth of several million dollars. He learned, during his residency (MD training), how to invest in real estate from a friend who owned multiple properties.

While we sipped an assortment of beverages together under the stars, Mervin told us, "A number of those rental properties are paid off. This gives me quite a bit of passive income." (Passive income is income for which you don't have to work.)

Mervin is a true expert on real estate. You may have come across "pundits" who teach you how to become wealthy buying real estate, while they themselves own none, or who teach about flipping homes (flipping means to buy, repair, and sell), piling on other forms of debt while asking for your money in return. The surprising truth is that people who have become wealthy by owning real estate don't need your money. I promise you that you will be far wealthier if you follow advice from someone like Mervin rather than a pundit asking you for your money.

Let me share with you what I learned from Mervin while we camped that night.

## IS YOUR HOUSE AN INVESTMENT?

First, it is crucial to note that buying a house to live in is not an investment. Your friends, parents, or some financial advisers will show you statistics demonstrating how real estate has increased in value in the United States over long periods of time. I do not deny this fact. It is also essential to have a roof over your head, and on many occasions, it may be ideal to pay a mortgage instead of paying rent, or vice versa, provided you are in a financial position to do so.

But never buy a house just because it's going up in value. (Refer to the section on market bubbles in the previous chapter.) And just because you can afford one doesn't necessarily mean you should buy one. It is better to reflect on whether or not you need one.

If you can afford a house, and you find it comfortable for yourself and your family, by all means, go ahead. Never buy a house that you cannot afford. As a rule of thumb, mortgage payment +

insurance + tax + HOA + maintenance = current rent payment you can afford + reasonable dollar amount. A reasonable dollar amount is money you can afford to lose every month without a change in your lifestyle or savings; ideally the more minimal the better.

The second crucial rule: flipping a house is not an investment and not an ideal route to building wealth unless you have enough disposable income (enough money for all expenses, if you are unable to sell the remodeled house) and are not over-leveraged (you have not borrowed so much that you are unable to pay back). Flipping houses is similar to trading stocks. It is as if you bought an undervalued piece of real estate, put in the effort to bring it up to market value in a short span of time, and sold it at a profit.

As long as you can flip houses without being over leveraged, you could make a substantial amount of money—provided you have the temperament to withstand gut-wrenching price moves in a volatile bear market (a crash in real estate prices), when real estate ceases to be as liquid (able to be sold or bought quickly) as it is when the economy is doing great. Not being over-leveraged and having enough disposable income are key to surviving downturns. Another way for you to enjoy building wealth may be to partner up with a friend or colleague who knows how to build, construct, or fix properties.

This has been Mervin's preferred way.

You can offer to put up cash, and your friend can contribute their skills and fix up a property, which can then be sold, with the profits divided. It's a win-win situation for both parties.

Real estate is unique in this way. One can be innovative and force appreciation (increase the value of real estate by making it nicer through effort) and build massive wealth this way. This is something you cannot do in the stock market. You cannot create or force appreciation into your stock holdings.

## REAL ESTATE AND TAXES

Always, when possible, buy rental real estate. It could be a single-family home, a multi-family home, or commercial real estate. Buying rental real estate has multiple advantages from an investment standpoint. First, you unlock all the tax advantages associated with this kind of real estate—depreciation expense, interest write-off, maintenance expense write-off, HOA fee write-off, property tax write-off, and many more. I am not a tax expert. I would encourage you to sit down with your tax advisor and discuss whether or not owning real estate is the right strategy for you.

So don't just buy real estate because someone told you it helps you lower your taxes. You should buy real estate because it's a good investment for you, not because you save on taxes or for another XYZ reason.

## CASH FLOW

If you bought a single-family home and rented it out, that means you invested in real estate; but it does not mean it's a good or bad investment.

Really? How do you then decide?

There were many people buying homes in 2006, just two years before the real estate market crashed in 2008, wiping out the savings of many hardworking people. Those people buying homes in that market could not differentiate between good and bad investments.

What makes an investment good or bad is its cash flow.

What is cash flow?

If a business generated $100 in earnings or revenue and spent $90 on expenses and was left with $10, then that $10 represents a positive cash flow.

Similarly, if the business earned $100 and had an expense of $120, now you're negative $20 (also called negative cash flow).

For example, let's assume you buy a single-family home for $100,000 and you receive a monthly rent of $1,000.

Hold on, where are you finding houses for $100,000, and who is paying you rent of $1,000?

These numbers are simplified for representation purposes. I intend to show you something profound.

In order to purchase the house, you will need to come up with 20 percent, which is $20,000, and the bank will lend you $80,000. Now remember, don't be cheap, and don't listen to pundits who tell you to buy real estate with 100 percent financing and borrow even the $20,000 with things like your credit card, etc. It's dumb and stupid advice.

This $20,000 should come from your savings. That means if you lose your $20,000, it should not affect your life. So remember as a starter, do not buy real estate with 100 percent OPM (other people's money/loan/debt) until you develop reasonable expertise at not losing yours and someone else's money. Never place your family's future in jeopardy by inculcating bad habits of excess debt or by becoming greedy. Don't be a Superhero. Don't try to hit a home run off the first ball you face.

Now let's crunch the numbers. Basically, on a $100,000 investment, you are making a return of $1,000 per month, therefore $12,000 a year, which makes a rate of return of 12 percent.

It might sound like, "If you bought a $100,000 house with full cash of your own, you make a 12 percent return."

But this situation is not quite that simple. Out of the $12,000 annual income, you need to pay property taxes, which are roughly 1–2 percent of the price of the property. You also need to deduct insurance and maintenance expenses, and maybe property management fees, etc., to come to your net income. Roughly, after all expenses, you may be left with about $8,000–$9,000 in net income if your property is in good shape. For calculation purposes, let's keep it simple. Let's say you receive $9,000 in pretax income, which is a 9 percent return.

That's not bad, especially if your savings bank account pays less than 1 percent a year.

Remember you will be able to write off expenses like property taxes, insurance, maintenance, management fees, etc., which will enhance your rate of return; but we shall stay away from these, for now, to keep the calculation simple.

Now what happens if you borrowed 80 percent and used 20 percent of your own money?

Why would I want to borrow money and pay additional interest on the borrowed money? That makes no sense.

But let's do a little mental exercise.

The post-expense income will be around $9,000, from which I will now deduct an additional expense called interest on the borrowed money (an interest rate of 3.5 percent in the current environment), which is around $230 per month × 12 months = $2,760.

So you will pay an annual interest expense of $2,760.

Now your new after-expense income is $9,000 − $2,760 = $6,240.

The first time I did this mental exercise I was upset that my new income was lower. You might also be wondering: why in the world would someone borrow money and increase their own expense by paying interest?

Here is why you would want to do that.

Remember your initial investment was only $20,000, therefore your return of $6,240 is 31 percent of $20,000. Yes, this is not a mistake!

Of course, some amount of mortgage payment goes into paying down the principal of the mortgage, increasing your equity in the real estate. After all your monetary obligations, what is left behind will be your free cash flow which, when divided by your initial investment, gives you a number called cash-on-cash return. Let's not go too much into numbers and details. I'm keeping things simple to make sure the concept is clear.

Essentially when you bought a property with all of your money, you made a 9 percent return. But when you used 80 percent of *someone else's* money, you made a 31 percent return.

The first time I learned this I felt like a bulb lit up in my head. The major takeaway: leverage (borrowing money to buy a positively cash flowing property) apparently enhances the rate of return!

## INFINITE MONEY

There are two types of debt: good and bad. Bad debt is debt that you have to pay by working. Some examples are credit card debts, car loans, student loans, etc. Good debt is debt that someone else pays for you, for instance debt on rental real estate, which is paid from rental income.

As you may have analyzed so far, the same investment, when bought with 20 percent of your money and 80 percent of someone else's money, enhances the returns from 9 percent to a whopping 31 percent. The less your own money goes into an outstanding investment, the higher your return. For example, $6,240 divided by zero dollars of yours invested is equal to infinity.

This, my friend, is called the *concept of infinite returns*. In simple words, it's creating money out of thin air.

"Money from thin air!" is what I exclaimed when Mervin explained this to me. Up until that day I had always worked for money, but after hearing his words, I realized that money could not only work for me but could also be created from thin air. Before then my thinking was: x number of patients and y number of hours will make me z amount of money to buy such-and-such a luxury.

But after rewiring my mind to adopt Mervin's advice, my thought process became: I could work x hours to save y amount to buy z property/asset. Then I could use the rent/income from z to buy a nice luxury. My luxuries would be paid by z asset and not my x hours. I could gradually replace these x hours with family time, vacations, and other important things that really make a life wonderful. Mervin uses his time and his rental income to do the things that he loves, like driving fast cars and partying.

Take a moment to imagine breaking this work cycle, this slavery cycle of the rat race, not only for yourself but also for your children and your children's children. Imagine a life in which you do not have to exchange your time for money, a pathway you could use to make yourself independent of the "work-money-expense-work" slavery cycle. Imagine your work being replaced with assets (property, stocks, bonds, and other investments), which paid (rent, dividend, premium, etc.) you to take care of your expenses. Ultimately, you could replace all your work income with asset income to pay all your expenses, and then you would never need to work again. This is the wisdom of the wealthy.

This concept of infinite returns can be similarly applied to stocks. You may choose to own a good company stock. Once the stock value goes up, you may choose to sell some of it, to take your initial investment out. The stock still left in your ownership is now an infinite return. With your initial investment back, essentially you have gained the leftover stock ownership for free.

Similarly, if you bought stock from your rental income or used your dividend income to buy more assets, your return on the new asset you bought is infinite.

Once you own your first property, let's say you choose to buy your second one with 80 percent bank money and 20 percent money of your own, borrowed from a line of credit on the first property. What's really happening is that your second property is completely bought from 100 percent credit, i.e., bank money, providing you an infinite return. Basically, the interest on the 80 percent of the second property loan is paid for by the second property's rental income, and interest on the 20 percent portion of the second property loan is paid for by the first property's rental income. Now this is what I call *magic*!

But before you jump into buying just any house on the market, let me warn you of the pitfalls that all early investors make while investing in real estate. These are things I learned, thanks to Mervin, who claims to be the "master of mistakes."

## TIPS TO AVOID PITFALLS WHILE INVESTING IN REAL ESTATE

**Tip one:** as exciting as the concept of infinite return sounds, never buy your first real estate investment with zero down, or 100 percent financed with someone else's money.

If you do not have the discipline to set aside money for emergencies, and if you do not have the discipline to save 20 percent cash to buy your first property deal, then you are not ready to invest in real estate. First you need to put some cash aside in case of any emergency.

What kind of emergency? And how much money should you put aside for emergencies?

Think of a straightforward emergency like losing your job. I learned my first lesson the hard way. I lost my first job, then wondered how I would pay my mortgage, car payments, and other expenses, etc. If you have a family, it's important to keep them safe and secure, and to be able to put food on the table for at least two to three months until you find another source of income. After saving for an emergency fund, save extra with the intention of buying your first investment, that is, toward the 20 percent. That's how you start.

**Tip two:** do your due diligence while working out finances. Analyze the expected rent to be received every month; figure out the market value of the property and the expected return with and without leverage. If you cannot make sense of the numbers or expected returns, educate yourself more on the topic of real estate. Beware of vacancies that can bite into your income, or situations like a financial crisis or the current COVID-19 pandemic. Some tenants lose their jobs and are unable to make rent payments. Beware of hidden HOA fees and county/city assessments.

Remember that real estate is not as liquid as stocks are. If you buy a bad stock or make an error in your analysis of future earnings, you can sell a stock immediately. Real estate is not so easy. It has additional costs, such as what you pay your real estate broker (commissions), and you could potentially incur other expenses like closing costs, etc.

**Tip three:** it doesn't matter how good a property is and how reliable the rent payer's credit is. If you overpay for a piece of real estate, your expected return could be poor or even negative. If you make a mistake in calculating a return and end up with negative cash flow, for the duration you own the property, you will have to keep putting money into the property to sustain the expenses. You will then own a liability and not an asset, because you are paying for it and it's not paying you.

**Tip four:** the beauty of real estate is you can do what is called a like-kind exchange. Roll over your capital gains from a property sold into a new property you want to buy, and defer taxes. I would recommend you ask your tax advisor about the 1031 exchange.

**Tip five:** follow these two simple rules:

- Rule 1: never compromise on educating yourself, and never lose money.
- Rule 2: follow Rule 1.

# Chapter 5

# MONEY MANAGEMENT

Now that you are familiar with the wisdom of the wealthy, let's talk action. The key to building and sustaining a wealthy life is money management. Follow the steps I've laid out for you ahead, and you'll be golden.

## 1) THE FIRST STEP TO MANAGING MONEY IS TO SAVE SOME.

If you have a job, do not quit your job. Do not listen to pundits who recommend quitting to chase after wealth. Make a detailed list or spreadsheet of how much you bring home every month and how much money is spent and on what things. Track every detail, including things like mortgage and student-loan payments.

Once you have all your income and expenses down, calculate your savings by subtracting your expenses from your income. Your household expenses are bills that need to be paid in order for you to live a life or to continue to live the way you live.

That is: all monthly income, less all monthly expenses, equals monthly savings.

Figure out how you can cut or minimize your expenses.

If your income and expenses are equal, and you are living paycheck to paycheck, and you are unable to cut your expenses, you will need to bring home more money, either with extra work or another job, a raise, promotion, etc.

The goal is to ensure you earn more and spend less so you can save some money.

If you have been able to save some money, you have accomplished Step 1.

## 2) PUT ASIDE MONEY FOR AN EMERGENCY, AND BUY TERM LIFE INSURANCE IF YOU HAVE A FAMILY TO SUPPORT.

Once you have started saving money, put aside enough to pay for household expenses, for at least three months, in case of an emergency such as losing your job.

If you support a family, buy term life insurance so they'll be taken care of if, God forbid, you leave this world earlier than expected.

### 3) GET OUT OF DEBT AS SOON AS YOU CAN.

If you've managed 1 and 2, then at this stage, there is no good debt or bad debt for you. All debt is bad debt until Step 5. After you have saved for emergencies, focus on your smallest debt, such as credit card debts, car loans, etc., and pay it off in full.

At this point, if you still have trouble cutting your expenses, consider destroying your credit cards, and start using cash.

Why cash?

Psychologically speaking, when you see "Benjamin Franklins" leave your hand, every time you spend money, you will really change your behavior. A credit card deprives you of this feedback; hence you tend to spend more, with a credit card, than you would with cash.

It's important to note that, once you have paid off your smallest debt, you no longer have a payment on that loan; your savings are higher.

Now find the next smallest loan and attack it until you have paid it off in full.

Repeat these steps until all debts are paid off and the only debts you have left are your home mortgage and/or student-loan debt. (Note: it's not necessary to pay off your home mortgage or student loans to move to Step 4, though you can if you want to or are able to.)

## 4) SAVE MONEY TO INVEST, THAT IS, TO BUY ASSETS.

After paying all your debts, your savings should go into investing or buying assets.

You need discipline here. Do not buy liabilities. (Remember that liabilities are things you pay for, and assets are things that pay you.)

You can start by using your savings to buy dividend-paying ETFs (electronically traded funds).

As you save more, buy more dividend-paying ETFs and stocks/bonds, etc.

(The ideal way to do it is to use your retirement accounts like 401(k)s/IRAs. I also recommend buying assets, in your traditional brokerage accounts, after you have maximized your retirement accounts.)

## 5) SAVE MONEY TO BUY INCOME-PAYING REAL ESTATE AS AN ASSET.

Do not buy land or a piece of real estate that does not pay you income.

Do not buy a second home or vacation home (liabilities).

What you need to buy is income-paying rental real estate.

Save 20 percent for a down payment, and borrow 80 percent from the bank, which would be considered good debt.

Do not buy rental real estate until you have completed and surpassed Step 4 with discipline.

## 6) REPEAT STEP 4 AND STEP 5, UNTIL YOUR NET-ASSET INCOME EVERY MONTH SURPASSES YOUR ENTIRE MONTHLY HOUSEHOLD EXPENSES.

Net-asset income = asset revenue (rent, dividend, interest, premium, etc.) minus asset expense (interest on asset loans, maintenance of properties, taxes on assets, etc.).

At this point you have attained financial independence.

At this point you no longer have to work to live a life.

At this point you are free from the financial slavery cycle of money problems.

## 7) GROW YOUR NET ASSET INCOME TO BUY THE THINGS THAT MAKE LIFE FUN!

Get that second vacation home or that Porsche you always wanted.

At this point you would have attained financial freedom. You may choose to do whatever you want with your time. You can quit your job, if you want to, and follow your heart. Follow your passion, travel the world, or just sip cocktails on a beach.

## 8) CHANGING THE WORLD.

Remember, you don't have to quit your job to start a company that becomes a billion-dollar company someday. You just need enough chances to test your ideas as an entrepreneur, to turn them into billions in a failproof manner. If you quit your job without reaching Step 6 or Step 7, then you are just placing your family's future in jeopardy if you fail. That is not smart. But if you have reached Step 6 or 7, you have nothing to lose if your endeavor fails. You can start, again and again and again, until you have changed the world. No matter what the outcome of your endeavor, your family does not have to go to bed hungry or stressed. If you are dedicated, you can get to Step 6 or 7 in five to six years or earlier. If, like me, you are not a big fan of sipping a cocktail on the beach, you will want to change the world. Who is in a better position to change this world than you, whose cost to do so is zero. At Step 7, I know you may want to just sip cocktails on a beach, for the rest of your life, but I hope you change this world for the betterment of all humanity. Best of Luck!

## WORDS THAT CHANGED MY LIFE

Back at the campfire in northern Minnesota, I sipped my coffee, looked at the sky, and marveled at the hours of invaluable advice I had received. How lucky I was to sit with people wiser than myself, to have acquired so much wisdom from Masood, Mervin, and Ravi! I was fortunate that our paths had crossed. Today, because of these wise men and their wisdom, I have learned to transmute success and become wealthy. Now wishing success, wealth, and freedom for you, I offer this wisdom to you.

# APPENDIX

Short (selling) is the opposite position of long (buying) a stock. One makes money when it is anticipated that a market or a stock/ETF, etc., will go down in value. It is usually done by selling a borrowed stock—or ETF, etc.—that belongs to someone else. One doesn't necessarily have to own a stock to sell short.

With a long or buy position on a stock, you make money if you buy low and sell high. With a short or sell position on a stock, you sell first at high, wait for the market to go down, and then come back and buy low. The difference is your profit.

There are always some so-called heroes who successfully "short" one or two companies and make money by a fluke, and they will always brag about it.

What they don't talk about is the time when this choppy market rallied (when a market or stock goes up in value significantly) against them, and they lost more money.

What they also never seem to talk about is that, while performing this heroic task of shorting, they pissed their pants in fear a little too.

Most veteran stock market traders know that shorting, without owning or betting that a particular stock or group of companies will lose value, is profitable only in the short term; it is kind of a stressful event, so stressful that they wake up, several times at night, to check and make sure their decisions were correct.

Some traders reduce this stress by placing proper stop-losses. These are protective instruments: if a stock or ETF reaches a certain value, the computer automatically closes that position before the loss grows. They hope the stock doesn't gap across against you without hitting the stop-loss, that is, the stock doesn't jump the stop-loss, during extreme market moves, in which case the stop-loss instrument would have failed.

Sometimes the stock collapses, it goes down in value, and the "short" selling stock trader makes money.

Sometimes it doesn't.

And sometimes shorting "dirty company stock"—fake companies

or market bluffs who pretend to innovate but are bluffing—is a very successful strategy.

But let me be clear: shorting the market is not the path to wealth.

What is worth more, your sleep or the stress-filled couple of bucks on which you owe short-term capital gains? (Capital gains are taxes you owe to the IRS if you made a profit trading stocks, etc.)

Or, how about having a heart attack from all the stress that comes from losing all that money at a very young age? Is it worth it?

Remember, most pundits or self-proclaimed gurus or professionals, who teach you how to short the market, make money "teaching" you how to "short," and not from shorting the companies (stocks) in the market themselves.

If you are a person who shorts stocks, and you short a company that is not a bluff, you are essentially betting against the spirit of innovation that exists in the hearts of those people who created and run that company.

And if you find a person still betting against the spirit of human innovation, after you have read this book, then please give that person a pack of adult diapers.

If you bet against the spirit of human innovation, the odds are against you. If you believe you can bet against the spirit of human innovation and win, lord have mercy on you.

If you are shorting companies that are not bluffs, you are basically gambling for fun, while knowing that the odds are against you. If you call that investing, you are only deceiving yourself.

There is basically no difference between someone sitting at a casino slot machine, gambling his savings away, and this strategy for investing.

If you are still interested in shorting, then use a proper trail stop, or maybe buy a "put" option instead. Good Luck!

## SECTION 2
## PUMP-AND-DUMP SCHEMES

Some pundits buy a stock first; then on TV, social media, etc., they promote a single stock. When enough people hear the news, they rush into buying that particular stock. When enough people buy it, that particular stock goes up in value. The original pundit sells his stock at a higher price and gets out of his position while encouraging others to continue to buy or hold the stock. Usually, people who listened to the pundit are left holding the bag when the stock collapses.

## SECTION 3
## FOR ADVANCED INVESTORS

Investing in the stock market, without understanding derivatives, places you at a significant disadvantage.

Note: my hope with the information I am conveying through this book is to help improve your general knowledge. It's not investment advice in itself. I am not an investment advisor. In addition, this is not the only successful approach to investing. The reader is not obligated to read or follow the advice. This section is for education only. Furthermore, using this approach, one may make or lose money. The author takes no responsibility for your losses and seeks no percentage of your profits. Profitability relies on individual wisdom of the markets, knowledge, and understanding. It is the responsibility of the reader of this book to acquire more education on topics discussed in this book for better understanding of the information presented.

**Options** are financial instruments that are derivatives based on the value of underlying securities, such as stocks or ETFs.

One can buy an option or sell an option.

Buying an option is called "being long the option," and selling an option is called "being short the option."

There are two types of options: put options and call options.

Premium is the price paid or received for buying or selling an option.

Strike price is the specified price at which an option is exercised.

In **options** trading, "to **exercise**" means to put into effect the right to buy or sell the underlying security (stock, ETF, commodity, etc.) that is specified in the **option** contract.

A call option is **in the money** (ITM) if the market price is above the strike price.

A put option is **in the money** if the market price is below the strike price.

A call option is OTM (out of the money) if the underlying price is below the strike price.

A put option is OTM if the underlying's price is above the strike price.

A **put option** is a contract that gives its holder the right to sell a set number of stocks, ETFs, etc., at a specific price, called the strike price, before a certain expiration date. If the **option** is **exercised**, the seller of the **option** contract is obligated to purchase the shares from the **option** holder.

A **call option** gives you the right, but not the requirement, to purchase a stock at a specific price (known as the strike price) by a specific date, at the **option's** expiration. For this right, the **call** buyer will pay a premium, which the **call** seller will receive.

## HOW CAN OPTIONS BE YOUR ADVANTAGE?

You can buy put option contracts, to protect your stock investments against market declines; sell put option contracts, to take stock or ETF allotments at lower prices; and sell call option contracts, in order to sell stocks or ETFs at a specified higher, profitable price and to lower your cost of stock/ETF ownership.

## HOW TO USE OPTIONS IN COMBINATION WITH STOCK/ETF OWNERSHIP

"Position" means your stock or ETF position.

A long position means you have bought the underlying stock or ETF, etc.

A short position means you have sold the underlying stock or ETF, etc.

## SELLING NAKED

Ravi said, "Sell naked puts."

Selling a naked put is the act of selling an uncovered put option.

(An uncovered option position is defined as an option position that has been initiated without a prior stock or ETF position.)

For example, if you were short 100 stock and sold a put contract, that position would be called a covered put.

Similarly, if you were long 100 stock and you sold a call option, that position would be called a covered call.

"Options are risky. Aren't they?" I asked.

Ravi continued. "Now this is one aspect of investing that the pundits call risky and advise you to never do, because it's their top strategy to beat the market. If they told you everything about the market, how would they make money off of you?"

Remember, every investment is risky if you do not understand it. You could buy a single-family house and rent it out and still lose money. You could buy a stock and it might go to zero. There are a million ways to lose money. But with the right approach, you will come out ahead.

When selling naked puts, always sell cash-secured ones; never sell them on margin (money you have to borrow from brokerage because your account has insufficient money).

If you sell a naked put, on margin (borrowed money), and the market happens to move against you—and sometimes it moves quickly against you—you will be caught swimming naked (trading in the stock market, with insufficient money, or trading the market on borrowed money).

## MERVIN MARGIN ERROR

Mervin laughed and said, "I have learned it the hard way. I have received many margin calls. Once, the brokerage company force-sold my stock and ETF holdings at a substantial loss. Don't make the mistakes I made. If I had not made these mistakes, my net worth would be a lot higher today. So never sell or buy (options) on margin; always sell a cash-secured one."

Margin call happens when you trade on borrowed money from a brokerage firm. If things go wrong, you will need to come up with more money. If not, your brokerage firm will force-sell your stock holdings and other assets to raise more cash. It is a common cause for massive losses in the stock market.

"What happens when the market moves against me?" I asked.

Ravi said, "You mean, what happens when your short/sold put option is in the money. Let's explore this together. There is an XYZ stock or ETF priced at, say, $100, and you happen to sell a cash-secured, naked put at a strike price of $70. The market moves against you, or the stock/ETF value goes down to, say,

$65. This means that your option position is in the money (ITM), and you will have to take the allotment of the stock at $70, when your option contract expires, or sooner."

Mervin said, "Let me ask you this. If this happened and you were allotted or obligated to buy this stock/ETF for $70, what would be so bad about that?"

I replied, "Well the stock EFT is now $65, and I have a paper loss (non-real loss) of $5. What good is that?"

Ravi said, "Remember, you did not directly buy the stock with $100 of your cash; instead, at that time, you sold a put. Now because it was exercised, you were given stock at $70. Also remember you received a premium (payment for selling an option contract) when you sold a put. Now considering you had bought the stock at that time for $100, then with the same event unfolding, you would be sitting on a paper loss of $35 on each stock."

Ravi asked, "Did that make sense?

"Let me explain again. If you had xxx dollars in your account and you sold a naked put at a strike price of $70, you receive a premium for the sale of option, and furthermore, you bought a good stock or ETF at a $30 discount. Had you bought it at $100, then you would have lost $35 on every stock, because the current price of the stock is $65."

I said, "This sounds like a win-win scenario. Why doesn't everyone do it or talk about it? What if the stock never came down and hovered around $100 or went up?"

Ravi smiled. "Then you just keep the premium collected for selling the option contract. At expiration, the contract disappears and then you just rinse and repeat."

I could feel my heartbeat speeding up.

Ravi continued. "Selling a naked put will always place you at the advantage of buying a good company at a lower price."

If you sold a put, and if your put is in the money, then for the premium you received, you are obligated to receive a certain stock/ETF at the agreed-upon strike price.

Also, if you happen to have bought a put, then for the premium you paid, you will have the right to give away your stock to someone else at the agreed upon strike price. In simple terms, if you sold a put and the stock/ETF went up, you would have made money. If you bought a put and the stock/ETF went down, you would have made money.

You would want to buy a put option if you own some stock and you expect or are worried that the stock market could crash because, if that happens, you can still sell your stock at the higher strike price agreed upon in the option contract.

Essentially if you sold a put and the market crashed, that means you will have to buy that stock at the strike price. Remember, you get paid premium to sell an option, but you pay a premium to buy an option.

Mervin smiled and said, "So if you get paid to buy a stock that you want to own anyway, especially at a lower price, why would you not do it?"

The investing approach of the wealthy just makes sense.

Suppose you sell a naked put, at a certain strike price, and the stock value goes down drastically, because of some bad news or poor earnings report. In a manner, you now have significant paper losses (non-real losses), even after the stock was allotted at a lower price.

Sure, this can happen on many occasions. It's not all sunshine and rainbows. But remember, if you had outright just bought the stock to begin with, you would not have received any premium. You would have lost more money, because you bought at a higher price and the stock went down, drastically. There is no replacement for due diligence; without it you will be eaten by a lion. This is where fundamental analysis, and the analysis of the future prospects of a company, are so essential. If you are worried about individual companies, then just stick with ETFs.

## COVERED CALLS

Selling covered calls is another exciting way to lower your purchase cost. You can sell covered calls on your existing positions (stock/ETF ownership). In fact, I believe it may be the ideal way to sell stock ownership at a profit. For example, if you own a one hundred stock/ETF of XYZ, you could then sell one call option against that position and collect a premium for a future predetermined price of sale (strike price) of your stock/ETF.

Say, for example, on a stock that is selling at $100, you can sell a call option at $120 strike price. Once your option is in the money, your stock is sold for $120, making you a profit of $20 on each stock; plus remember the premium you collected selling the call. If the strike price is not reached and the stock hovers around $110 or stays below $120, at the time of call option expiration, you get to keep your stock and your collected premium. You can now sell more calls in the future to collect more premium, until the event of your call option being in the money happens and your stock is sold at a profit to you. How wonderful is this strategy? you may wonder. It is also important to note that, until this event (stock disposition) occurs, you own your stock; so you will continue to receive the dividends if paid by the respective stock/ETF you own.

## SMALL PROFIT IS STILL BETTER THAN NO PROFIT

One might wonder, "What if I sold a covered call on my position and collected a premium? But immediately after I sold the option, the stock just rallied (went up in value) and rallied like hell. I would end up selling my stock at a smaller profit, while I could have sold at an outstanding profit if I never initiated a covered call."

This happens to many of us. If this event happens, it's always good. What is important, however, is to buy low and sell high. Now you have indeed sold high, just maybe not very high. One can never lose money, taking profits.

## HOW TO HEDGE YOUR STOCK POSITIONS

It's extremely important to protect and minimize your downside, which you have done by buying low (via selling cash-secured puts) and collecting consistent premiums (by selling covered calls). Sometimes I use part of the premium collected to hedge my stock positions; this is done by buying put options. So, if suddenly the market crashed tomorrow, I would not lose money, because with a put option I have the right to sell my stock at the strike price (the previous, higher price, which existed before the crash happened).

This means I can still get out of the market (sell my stock), at yesterday's price, even though the market has crashed and burned to ashes today.

That, my friend, is the wisdom of the wealthy, the art of always protecting what you own.

It's important to hedge (protect your stock positions), especially in a low-volatility environment when there is a high mathematical probability of an adverse event happening.

Low volatility: when the market is not expected to have too many big up-or-down moves.

High volatility: when a market is expected to have very big, and many, up or down moves.

In a low-market-volatility environment, most market participants (traders and investors) become complacent. Participants think the market will continue to go up forever.

It is precisely during periods of low volatility that you should consider buying a put option.

Also, during low-volatility periods, the option premiums are cheaper to buy.

## SHORT CALL DANGER

Most importantly, remember, never sell a naked call option on margin or borrowed money.

This could potentially make your losses infinite.

What I mean by that is if you sold a call at $120 strike price and the stock started rallying (increasing in value), then your call option will become in the money (ITM).

So you are now obligated to sell/short stock, which you did not previously own, at $120.

The scary question is, what if this stock continues to rally and goes to $1,000 or, say, $2,700?

An event like this could place you in a very precarious position. You should never want to be on the wrong side in a disaster.

Selling a naked call is a position equivalent to selling 100 stock short. This is similar to betting against the spirit of human innovation. One could lose all his clothes in doing so. Betting against the spirit of American innovation has never ever been a good idea and will never ever be one.

## THE CATCH

Keep in mind there are some guaranteed ways of getting caught swimming naked. To avoid losing all your clothes and your entire life savings, remember this.

Absolutely, do not sell naked options on margin.

Do not sell naked options with infinite risk.

Do not place complex option trades because some pundit on TV or your new friend made a YouTube video explaining such complex trades.

Some pundits may claim to have made a 50 percent or 70 percent return on capital by selling fancy instruments like spreads, collars, condors, strangles, and full wing/half wing or broken wing butterflies, etc. Remember, complex investment strategies are garbage strategies.

They sound fancy. But over a long period of time, they just turn out to be an even-sum game, minus the transaction costs. Eventually your net liquid portfolio (total money in your account) will be lower, and you will have made no money. Then you'll wonder if you should go back to simple dollar-cost averaging.

People have different investing strategies, but what has consistently made me money is this: I never sell options to generate cash alone, and I never sell them on leverage (borrowed money) to generate cash. I have always used option contracts to take allotment (buy stocks, ETF, etc., when exercised) at lower prices, ensure disposition (sell stocks, ETF, etc., when exercised) at higher prices, or hedge my existing positions (buying puts, using premium from selling covered calls) to protect what I own.

## PROTECTING YOUR PROFITS AND CAPITAL

If you have a stock position that has grown massively, over time, and it has now grown 200–300 percent, you are concerned and believe something could trigger a correction like, for example, an election or an international trade standoff, etc., whatever may be the cause of concern.

You will not be wrong if you purchase some put options to protect your existing positions.

If your perspective of the market is bearish (you think the market could crash) and you anticipate a correction (expect it to go down), you may even consider selling covered call options against your position and using the premium collected to buy put options. This will help you withstand the downturn and protect your capital.

This is the wisdom of the wealthy on how to make sure you protect your downside so that the upside can take care of itself.

From that day onward, I never looked at options as just risky instruments. As a matter of fact, their existence is a blessing for simple investors like you and me. Always use them, in combination with your long (bought) or short (sold) stock/ETF positions, to effectively execute your strategy.

Options are not risky; investing without learning the applications of options is risky.

## STRATEGIC EXECUTION EXAMPLES

This information is meant to demonstrate an example and serve the purpose of education only. It is not investment advice, and it in no way is meant to tell you to take or initiate any investment position on SPY, FB, or any other stock/ETF/bond, etc.

Liquid stock/ETF: stock/ETF that can be bought or sold easily because of the availability of many buyers and sellers for that particular stock or ETF.

This information is pulled out of the market. A liquid ETF SPY (S&P 500 index ETF), and a liquid Facebook stock (FB), are shown as examples.

May 6, 2020

Current VIX (volatility index) = 34.12

Contracts chosen with expiration 408 days out.

SPY is trading at $283 price per stock of ETF approx.

By selling a cash-secured put, at a strike price of $250, you will collect an 8.8 percent return on your cash. This option contract has a 70 percent probability of being out of the money.

If the ETF price dropped in value, then you got paid 8.8 percent for buying the ETF at $250 per ETF.

If the ETF did not drop in value, you simply get to keep 8.8 percent, in the form of premium, at the expiration of the option contract.

Suppose you decided to buy SPY at $283, then sell a covered call at a strike price of $325, again with a 70 percent probability of being out of the money. You would make a return (stock appreciation + premium collected) of 14.8 percent if the stock did rally (increase in value) and your option contract went in the money.

If the ETF did not rally (increase in value), you would still collect a 4 percent return on your stock, in the form of a premium, for selling a call option. You will also collect any dividends, and whatever appreciation, in the price of that ETF.

Furthermore, you will still own the ETF to sell more covered calls in the future.

FB is trading at $208 approx.

By selling a cash-secured put, at a strike price of $185, you will collect a 10.6 percent return on your cash on this naked put option, which has a 70 percent probability of being out of the money.

If FB's price dropped in value, then you got paid 10.6 percent for buying the stock at $185 per stock.

If FB's price did not drop in value, you simply get to keep 10.6

percent, in the form of premium, at expiration of the option contract.

Suppose you decided to buy FB at $208, then selling a covered call at $270 again, with a 70 percent probability of being out of the money. You would make a return of (stock appreciation + premium collected) 29.8 percent if the stock did rally and your option went in the money.

If the stock did not rally, you would still collect a 4.8 percent return on your stock, in the form of a premium, for selling a call option. You will also collect any dividends (on a dividend-paying stock only) and whatever appreciation in the price of the stock.

Furthermore, you will still own the stock to sell more covered calls in the future.

Note: your return will be higher in a single stock when compared to an ETF, as single stocks are more volatile than a collection of stocks like an index ETF.

A higher volatility generally means a higher premium for sellers and a higher cost for buyers.

## HOW TO BUY LOW AND SELL HIGH

Now what if you took an allotment of stock or ETF, via naked put, and then turned around and sold covered calls at a predetermined strike price?

You would have ensured and mastered the fundamental principle of any trade, which is to "buy low and sell high," effectively bypassing your own human psychological bias.

Lightning Source UK Ltd.
Milton Keynes UK
UKHW022025080822
407030UK00009B/202/J